W9-AQE-497

American
Negro Slavery
and Abolition
A Sociological Study

American Negro Slavery and Abolition

A Sociological Study

Wilbert E. Moore

UNIVERSITY OF DENVER

THE THIRD PRESS

JOSEPH OKPAKU PUBLISHING COMPANY, INC.
444 CENTRAL PARK WEST, NEW YORK, N.Y. 10025

ST. PHILIPS COLLEGE LIBRARY

326
M 825a

First Printing

copyright © 1971 by WILBERT E. MOORE

All rights reserved. Except for use in a review, the reproduction or utilization of this work or part of it in any form or by electronics, or other means, now known or hereafter invented, including xerography, photocopying, and recording, and in any information storage and retrieval system is forbidden without the written permission of the publisher.

Library of Congress Catalogue Card Number: 73–148362
SBN 89388–000–0

Printed in the U.S.A.

Designed by Barbara Kohn Isaac

Contents

29369

Preface

This book is now more than thirty years overdue. It is with some delight that I now offer for publication a scholarly work that could not have been published three decades ago. The original version of this book was submitted as a successful doctoral thesis in sociology at Harvard in January, 1940. At that time, sociologists rarely used historical materials (and they rarely do now). And, to my knowledge, whites did not approach American slavery dispassionately (and they rarely do now).

Circumstances do change. Many universities now have Black Studies Departments. African kingdoms will have to be rediscovered, African art newly found, and an awareness of African literature created.

Meanwhile what terms may one safely use with respect to that portion of the American population that is of Black African parentage? "Negro" is simply the Spanish or Portuguese word for

1

ST. PHILIPS COLLEGE LIBRARY

black and a legacy of Spanish and Portuguese entrepreneurs who made the slave-trade a New World phenomenon. The current term "Black," is an Anglicization of "Negro". From the position that "Black" is the contemporary version of the historical term "Negro," I shall use the traditional term "Negro" in this book purely because of the historical nature of the material and in order to avoid the confusion that might otherwise arise. The use of the term is purely descriptive.

In the original manuscript of this book I had written the following paragraph, which I consider to be still relevant today:

Upon numerous occasions in the course of preparing this thesis various persons have wanted to know its subject or inquired concerning the type of literature gracing my bookshelves. Following my general explanation, I have been asked one question more frequently than chance expectation would indicate: "What part of the South are you from?" Even in this day and age certain types of investigation seem to be set apart for those with particular family or sectional backgrounds. Of such qualifications for this study I have none. I am no grandson of a slaveholder; an obscure great-great-uncle was drafted into the Union Army in the Civil War. Beyond that there is a void. Of this absence of family or sectional interests in the controversy over slavery I make a positive virtue. For a study whose materials are historical and whose interest is scientific I make no apology for not having lived in the area with which it is principally concerned. Were the data contemporary, a different position and background might be necessary. One further word, however, may be added in view of the problem of the intrusion of extra-scientific interests upon scientific investigation. Although the attempt has been made throughout to maintain the necessary strict impartiality and I have not thought it necessary to gloss over or omit any relevant considerations, certainly my own ethical position may be stated, and possible unintended overtones thus discounted. Like the abolitionists, I find the idea of slavery incompatible with my ethical convictions.

This will be the last of the visible excerpts from my original prose. Some recent sources have been cited, but since the recent writers have primarily used the same sources as were originally at my disposal, I have made no exhaustive attempt at updating. One chapter of the original work "Slave Law and Social Structure," was published in *The Journal of Negro History,* Vol. 26, pp. 171–202, April 1941, and part of another chapter was adapted for joint publication with Robin M. Williams, Jr., upon whose independent work much of my interpretation relied. (See "Stratification in the Ante-Bellum South", *American Sociological Review,* Vol. 7, pp. 343–351, June 1942).

For encouragement in writing this book, I wish especially to record my warm thanks to Professor Joseph S. Himes of the University of North Carolina at Greensboro. He is a hero of mine, and I am delighted to be able to say so, and dedicate this book to Joe and his charming wife Estelle, who is also Joe's eyes.

WILBERT E. MOORE

Denver

I

Development and Sectional Segregation of American Negro Slavery

Whatever may have been said or written about the motives of English colonists in migrating to the New World—and the religious and political considerations are certainly not to be dismissed —these men were by no means so idealistic as to be averse to looking after their economic interests. After the first few struggling years, with a population barely maintained by fresh migrations, they set about finding ways and means of establishing a sound economy. Of land there was plenty, in fact, the surfeit of land precluded any marked division of labor and industrial organization. Any immigrant freeman preferred claiming and working his own land to wage labor for another.

INDENTURED SERVITUDE

The demand for labor consistently exceeded the supply. This was particularly true in Virginia, where almost at once tobacco became a commercial crop, most profitably grown on a large scale. The first attempt to solve this economic problem was the importation of indentured servants. Servitude was not a colonial invention; its English roots extended back to the Middle Ages, and its legal bases were primarily the apprenticeship and vagrancy laws.[1] Although the specific conditions of the indenture or servitude varied, as did the methods of recruiting—including kidnapping and transportation of convicts as well as concluding voluntary contracts—the principal features of the system were fairly uniform. The servant was transported to the colonies to serve some fixed number of years in payment for transportation and the services of the "entrepreneur." Unless transported directly by the intended employer or his agents, the trading company or ship captain sold the person's services to the highest bidder, in accordance either with the indenture contract, or, in the case of the unwilling immigrants, in accordance with local colonial legislation. Whether established by contract, legislation, or custom, the reciprocal rights and obligations of master and servant were fairly definite. By the purchase of the servant the master had claim to his services for the period of indenture. This work might be of any type demanded by the master, or, especially in the case of the willing migrants, for a specific technical, or even "professional" employment. The importation, under indenture, of school teachers and even preachers was not uncommon. Thus, no special social stigma attached to a period of servitude, once the servant was free of his obligations.[2] The master, in addition to paying the servant's passage through purchase of his indenture contract, was responsible for food and clothing, and, at the end of the term, for "freedom dues." The freedom dues consisted of payment in money or provisions intended primarily to assist the freedman in establishing his independence and to guard against his becoming a public charge.

The policy of indentured servitude was not a sectional one. The first Puritans in Massachusetts brought servants with them, and the corporation sent 180 of them for labor on the company's account.[3] These servants were viewed as not having "earned their keep," and the survivors were freed in 1630 to shift for themselves. Nevertheless the practice was continued on a private basis, and immigrants of means brought their servants with them. Other Northern colonies followed the same general development.[4]

Although the policy in regard to white servitude among the Puritans of New England was thus no different from that of the Cavaliers of the South, there quickly appeared differences in the relative importance of the same labor system in the different sections. In Virginia, and later in Maryland, Georgia, and South Carolina, farming was rapidly established on a commercial basis. The growing of exportable commercial crops—tobacco, rice, and indigo—made the shortage of labor acute, while in the Northern settlement, with the exception of Pennsylvania,[5] the demand was limited to the number required as domestic "hands" for labor on the small farms, and as artisans. (The Pennsylvania case is interesting because land-grants for freedmen were more generous, and, early on, the demand for industrial workers was greater than in New York or New England.)

In both North and South the economic question to the enterpriser (farmer, merchant, petty manufacturer) was not one of bond labor or free labor but that of bond labor or no labor. Both sections suffered a labor shortage, and in neither were the politicians or enterprisers too particular about who the workers were, or how they came to be there.

White servitude was a labor system of major importance chiefly in Virginia and Maryland and there especially during the middle half of the Seventeenth Century. The economic development of the Carolinas and Georgia got under way later, so that slave labor was from the beginning more important than indentured labor. In Georgia, convict labor was treated as indentured labor without contract; its importance was small in commercial undertakings. It is in Virginia and Maryland then that indenture and slavery may be seen in closest contemporary development.

White servitude in Virginia began with the establishment of Jamestown in 1607, became a full-fledged system by 1612 and continued with unabated vigor until roughly 1676. Its decline was definitely under way by 1726, but the system retreated only slowly before slavery until 1788.[6]

The number of servants imported was even greater, in proportion to the population, in Maryland, and its degree and length of resistance to the slavery system much greater. McCormac[7] thinks this was due to Maryland's border position—it adopted the plantation system of the South and the White labor system of the North. This, however, is no more than a half-truth. Although it is true that the ratio of servants to freemen or servants to slaves was higher—over a longer period—than in other colonies, at the peak period of the slave trade the White servants were outnumbered by Negro slaves by 4.8 to 1.[8] Gray notes that "probably a majority of White persons who immigrated to the Southern Colonies entered as servants . . ." [9] (indeed that is almost certainly true of all the "old settlers" before the American Revolution), and the limited duration of servitude steadily reduced the proportion of White servants relative to the permanent or life-time Negro slaves.

Until early in the nineteenth century, however, White servants continued to supply the need for artisans, workmen for small-scale manufacturing, and for directors and overseers of the slaves. The economic importance of White servitude during the colonial period was great. It was a profitable labor system. Why then did it ultimately give way before slavery?

From Servitude to Slavery

The contemporaneous development of the two systems of servitude and slavery and their relative advantages are pertinent to this question. Negroes were first introduced in Virginia in 1619, or perhaps 1620—that matters little: Until late in the seventeenth century the slave trade in Virginia and Maryland was of minor importance in comparison to the importation of White servants. Initially Negroes were not introduced *instead of* White servants, but simply *in addition to* indentured bondsmen, and their terms were fixed by local custom and legislation as were those of White servants involuntarily transported. The innumerable historians who give the year 1619 as the date for the introduction of slavery in the American colonies are simply wrong. Slavery came considerably later, as we shall see.

So long as Negroes were treated as bondsmen without written contract—and that situation generally held until 1661—the advantages of White servants over Negroes were obvious. At least a small proportion of the Whites had technical skills, most already knew the language, all knew the ways of Western civilization. There was a smaller loss in passage, and a much smaller loss in "seasoning." Negro servants then were definitely second-best, imported to help in filling the ever-present menial labor deficiency.[10]

The crucial turning point in the relative importance of the two classes of laborers came with their separation into different labor systems. Although as early as the 1640's some owners had adopted the practice of considering Negroes and the children of bound Negro women, as slaves for life, official recognition came slightly later. "Slaves" are first mentioned in Virginia laws in 1656, and by 1662 mulatto children born of slave women were required to follow the status of the mother.[11] This put the relative advantages of White and Negro bondage in a different light.

The establishment of slavery as the bondage system of Negroes obviously did not overcome the obvious advantage of White servitude. But it did add an economic advantage to Negro servitude for plantation labor, where the technical and racial advantage of the Whites was less relevant. The economic advantage of Negro slavery over White servitude, which was largely responsible for the ultimate ascendancy of slavery, rested upon a number of factors.

(1) It had not been customary to employ White women servants in field labor. "In this respect servitude was defective not only as a system of labor, but also as a system of immigration, for it favored the selection of men rather than of families." [12] The economy of the plantation system under slavery depended upon utilizing the labor of all to the fullest extent. (The argument is probably spurious, since it is not at all clear that White women or children were exempt from *all* labor at the time; many household tasks were available.)

(2) The cost of maintenance of slaves was slightly less than that of servants, principally because of the smaller amount and poorer quality of the clothes furnished to slaves.

(3) The cost of transportation of slaves was not much higher than for servants. It is true that the planter paid more for the slaves than for the servants, since the traders and middlemen could command a higher price for servants for life. This assured, however, a greater interest of traders in the slave trade than in the servant trade, and thus left a continuous supply less uncertain. Despite the difference in initial cost, Gray summarizes the advantage to the planter in purchasing the slave:

About the beginning of the eighteenth century a servant for a four-year term could be obtained for £10 to £15, while adult slaves could be had on the average for £18 to £20. The services of the slave were for life, as compared with four years for the servant, and the descendants of the slave would also belong to the planter. In spite of the cost of raising them, slave children were of some value at birth.[13]

It may also be noted that original inequality of price was at least slightly reduced by the fact that no "freedom dues" were involved in the slavery system.

(4) The slave was more completely under the master's control: no contract of indenture specified the type of labor, nor did the laws or custom grant the slave the right to legal complaint. It is thus understandable that the White servant was regarded as less "tractable" than the slave. The Negro slave was indeed more tractable for he had no ready escape from his bondage, and often had limited skills, including those of language.

(5) Finally, slavery had an economic advantage over White servitude in the greater difficulty of escape from bondage. The White servant "had no mark upon him" to distinguish him from a freeman. Once away from the immediate community where his status was known, his capture was unlikely. Slavery was the presumptive status of the Negro, and his color alone distinguished him.

It should again be noted that the transition from servitude to slavery in Virginia and Maryland was extremely slow. Although it may be correctly said that the establishment of slavery as the bondage system for Negroes forecast the termination of White servitude, that end was not immediate. As already indicated, the early advantage of slavery was primarily for plantation labor. Even there the transformation was dependent as such upon the completion of the terms of White servants, and, more importantly, upon the availability of imported slaves. This still left a demand for servants for all other types of work. However, these too gave way before slavery. While freshly imported African Negroes were capable only of unskilled physical labor in gangs under close supervision, two other sources of slaves reduced some of the disadvantages of the "seasoning" process. The first source of additional labor was the West Indies where the plantation and slavery system were already well established.[14] West Indian slaves were already "seasoned," or, accustomed to plantation labor and its routine, and partially familiar with the language. Some may have been taught technical skills, as well. With the complete displacement of White servitude the second source, the native-born children of imported slaves, was probably more important. These were reared in the system, and the master had the opportunity of increasing their intrinsic value by teaching them technical skills or training them for household or similar service. Once the last advantages of White servitude had been largely erased, the full establishment of the slavery system in its matured and complex form was simply a question of time and supply (which amounted to the same thing).

Thus, given a demand for labor in the English colonies, and given the abundance of land and possibility of independent self-sufficiency of the freeman, wage labor and indentured servitude became economically impractical. It has also been shown that there was a differential demand for labor, so that, of the earliest colonies, those in New England required relatively few laborers in comparison with Virginia and Maryland.

The policies of the colonies regarding White servitude being equal, the differential development of labor systems is to be explained in terms of divergent economic regimes. That indentured servitude was displaced by Negro slavery in the South can be explained by the economic advantages of slavery. The relatively smaller need of extra labor in the North, particularly the Northeast, together with an absence of the type of economic activity for which unskilled slave labor was fitted, prevented such an economic development from taking place.

Two sets of facts do not exactly square with this analysis; the demonstration cannot be quite so neat. The transition from White servitude to slavery was by no means automatic. It depended upon at least a minimal legalization and institutionalization of a labor system which, whatever its economic similarities to indentured servitude, was quite different institutionally. It follows that the considerations involved in the institutional change were not exclusively economic ones. Although Negro slavery did exist in the North during the colonial period, like indentured servitude, it did not become an economic system of major importance. Its mere existence merits specific note. The differential development of the labor system in the North and South was not, then, completely divergent. The economic analysis of the formative periods of both systems remains substantially correct, not in absolute terms, but in terms of relative importance, and one of the principal criteria of importance is that of the proportion of laborers in the total population. To this point the analysis will presently return.

EARLY REGULATION OF THE SLAVE TRADE

Before considering the statistics of slavery until the time of the complete divergence of the Northern and Southern labor systems, one further set of facts demands consideration. Even after the definite establishment of slavery as a labor system, neither the number of slaves imported, nor the conditions under which they were admitted was allowed to follow the automatic operation of the market. The large number of restrictions, levies, and prohibitions which were being continually passed, changed, relieved, and vetoed (by the English Government) are important not only to highlight some of the political and social difficulties in the establishment of a slavery system, but also because of the long-standing and erroneous interpretation of their significance.

In a chronological summary of legislation by the colonies concerning the slave trade, Du Bois lists 87 separate enactments, some of which were vetoed by the governors or other English officials.[15] Of those enactments listed 54 are simply an imposition of a duty, presumably for revenue purposes.[16] Other acts recite the dangers of a growing servile population and seek temporary relief, either through temporary or permanent prohibition, or through encouragement of the importation of White servants by means of smaller duties, freedom from duties, or outright bounties. The first "restriction" listed by Du Bois is the famous one of Massachusetts, enacted in the "Liberties of Forreiners and Strangers" in 1641, three years after the first introduction of Negroes into the colony. It follows:

There shall never by any bound slaverie villinage or captivitie amongst vs, unles it be lawful Captives taken in iust warres & such strangers as willingly selle themselves or are sold to us. And those shall have all the liberties & Christian usages wch ye law of god established in Jsrell concerning such p/sons doeth morally require. This exempts none from servitude who shall be judged there to by Authorities.[17]

In the light of the existence of slavery at the time and its continued existence, it is apparent that the exceptions provided in the law were quite ample to allow the buying and selling of slaves to continue. This act, however, was later often hailed by New England anti-slavery writers as proving the opposition of Massachusetts from the very beginning.

It is interesting that some of the colonial statutes placed a much smaller duty on freshly imported Africans than upon slaves sold from other colonies. This is to be explained by the well-established practice of selling criminal, rebellious, and recaptured runaway slaves out of the colony.[18]

The few cases of complete prohibition of slave importations, either by express act or by prohibitive duty, likewise involve factors other than deep-seated moral objections. The first evidence of this is the temporary character of each, and the failure of renewal. Of the situation in South Carolina and Georgia, Gray writes:

Prohibitive duties were in force for three years beginning July 5, 1741 (O. S.), for three years beginning July 16, 1747, and during the three years 1766 to 1768 inclusive. The enormous importations just before and just after the brief periods of restriction largely offset the effects of restraint and greatly enriched the speculative class, who, even as now understood how to make tariff changes redound to their profit. In fact, speculators were probably largely responsible for enactment of the restrictive act of 1765 and for the failure to continue it; and they profited largely from the imposition of the Georgia import duty in 1765 and from its repeal in 1768.[19]

Likewise in the case of import duties, aside from the interest in public revenue out of the profitable trade, Gray notes the following pressures at work:

About 1760 the question of import duties on slaves was largely a struggle in Virginia, as in South Carolina, between those who desired a high duty because already well stocked with slaves and those favoring low duties because of the desire to acquire more slaves.[20]

The net result of these considerations must be essential agreement with the conclusion of Gray:

It was long customary for Southern apologists to assert that the slave trade was forced upon the Southern colonies against their will, pointing to a long succession of statutes designed to tax the trade. There is no conclusive evidence, however, that before the middle of the eighteenth century these measures were due to any widely prevalent moral sentiment against the trade or to any conviction of its impolicy within moderate limits. The principal motives were fear of insurrection, desire for revenue, a speculative interest in increasing the prices of slaves already in the Colonies, dissatisfaction with the draining out of money, increase of colonial indebtedness, and a desire to prevent a retardation of the progress of the general body of slaves in civilization.[21]

The conclusion applies, moreover, equally well to the North, as shown in the previous reference to the famous Massachusetts act, and as becomes evident from the similar character of colonial legislation. As in the case of indentured servitude, therefore, it may be safely asserted that the colonial policy of the North in regard to slavery was not essentially different from that of the South.[22] But again, as in the case of bound White labor, the numerical proportion of slaves in the total population, and their importance in the regional economy, were quite different.

SLAVERY BECOMES PREDOMINANTLY SOUTHERN

Statistics of population size and composition in the colonial period are meager, inaccurate, and of slight comparability. An account of the differential development of the institution of slavery in the North and South must therefore be something less than statistically precise. This deficiency of exact information is fortunately not crucial for our purposes. The gross difference in the number and proportion of slaves in the North and South was so great after the very earliest introduction of slavery that the differences in estimates (or the frequent failure to distinguish the civil status of "Blacks"— their presumptive status being that of slaves) are inconsequential. The lack of adequate census materials does, however, prevent computation of reliable trends in slave population, and any sense, even crudely approximate, of the ratio of free Negroes to slaves. It will be recalled that since the original Negroes in the American colonies were treated as in temporary servitude, the lineage of "free men of color" may be about as long-standing as that of early White colonists, bond and free.

From a variety of sources it is possible to get some approximation of the number and proportion of slaves in the American colonies.[23] In the Northern colonies, the proportion of slaves may have approached 10% in Rhode Island and New Jersey at one or another period in the eighteenth century. The reported proportions in the same time span in such colonies as Virginia and South Carolina ran from around 40% to an incredible 70%. The proportions in North Carolina were always relatively low and in Georgia more or less steadily rising.

These estimates require further comment, however. Slavery was the putative status of Blacks toward the latter part of the eighteenth century, and census takers or estimators were not concerned about the civil status of Blacks (being insensitive both to the nuances of civil rights and the needs of future scholars), therefore the estimates of genuine slaves may have been inflated. That would be particularly true in the Northern colonies. Some, unknown, proportion of those registered as Negroes, Blacks, or slaves may well have been free Negroes.

The free Negro population in the North resulted from manumissions (an occurrence not unknown in the South), fugitives from the South and, descendants of early Negro bondservants. The true "underground railroad" was instituted later, but escape was by no means uncommon. We know that there were just over 6,000 slaves recorded in Massachusetts in 1790, but decisions based on the colonial constitution of 1780 [24] had abolished slavery in that colony by court decisions in 1783 and 1785. Still, black, free Negro, and slave seem to have been virtually interchangeable terms.

The continued failure to distinguish between slave and free Negro has wider significance than simple negligence or absence of modern census requirements. All Negroes certainly were not slaves, in any colony, and the legal status of the Negro who was a freeman was certainly nearer to the Whites than to the slaves. The failure to make a distinction between freeman and slave, while maintaining distinctions on racial grounds seems to conclude that in all the colonies slavery was the *presumptive* status of the Negro. Any person of color was first of all a Negro, therefore presumably a slave, and only accidentally a freeman.

When we remember that at least until just before the American Revolution there was no significant regional difference in the policy concerning the legality, justice, and morality of slavery, it is evident that the differential importance of that institution in the North and South during the colonial period was the result of divergent economies.

However, this view of the differential development of slave labor systems is defined in terms of relative importance, not of absolutes. Before passing to an analysis of free labor in the North and of the further development of slavery in the South, it is important to answer two questions: Why were there slaves in the North at all? When and why was slavery abolished there?

The answer to the first question is by no means simple, especially in view of the nearly universal agreement of authorities that slavery was "hopelessly unprofitable" in the North.[25] Any economic relationship which persists for two centuries in defiance of profit—especially when not imposed by an external power relation —is worthy of some attention. Negroes were first introduced as additional bonded servants, not as slaves. However, as in the South, once the status of the Negro became defined by law and custom as that of a slave, with the offspring belonging to the master, the system appeared more advantageous than White servitude. While it is true that slaves in the North were not used in large gangs, where their profitability was supposed to be greatest, neither were indentured servants. Wage labor was unprofitable in the days of plentiful land for any prepaid passenger; therefore, the system demanded support of a large serving class. Furthermore, the large and ever-increasing demand for labor in the South resulted in a continuous stream of fresh importations of "unseasoned" Africans who were not suitable for the kinds of labor required in the Northern colonies. The slaves brought to the Northern colonies were generally brought from the South or the West Indies.

The reasons were several. Small parcels, better suited to the retail demand, might be brought more profitably from the sugar islands whither New England, New York and Pennsylvania ships were frequently plying than from Guinea whence special voyages must be made. Familiarity with the English language and the rudiments of civilization at the outset were more essential to petty masters than to the owners of plantation gangs who had means for breaking in fresh Africans by deputy. But most important of all, a sojourn in the West Indies would lessen the shock of acclimatization, severe enough under the best of circumstances.[26]

It is at least conceivable that, at the outset, slave labor in the North was not as unprofitable as the conventional interpretation would have it, but that the large-scale labor system of the plantation did not, and could not, be established. It is also highly probable that slaves were a kind of conspicuous consumption for prosperous merchants and officials. Much of Roman slavery was also not economically profitable, but a mark of distinction. Southern slaveholders were not above this sort of status-seeking and some undoubtedly impoverished themselves by keeping a retinue of retainers that they could ill afford.

Although no exact figures are available, it is probable that the majority of slaves in the North were engaged in some type of "domestic service." The proportion so engaged seems to have been greater in New England than in the Middle Colonies. Sutherland, however, notes certain further tendencies and adds another interpretation. Except in Massachusetts, where census returns for Negroes were not made,

. . . not only had the most populous white towns the largest number of slaves but . . . the percentage of Negroes was considerably higher in the larger communities than it was in the small ones. Classic Puritan frugality offers the most obvious explanation, for New England slaves were used as house servants rather than as agricultural laborers. But the location of the towns and the proximity and development of the shipbuilding industry affords a sounder reason. Inland communities had few blacks, regardless of population size, but merchants who invested in shipping and in the Negro trade appear to have availed themselves of opportunities to employ slave labor. ". . . To the purely agricultural community, it is quite possible that the Negro contributed nothing; on the frontier, he disappeared entirely, for the average pioneer could not afford slaves." [27]

It is by no means obvious that the concentration of shipbuilding interests in larger towns is an especially good explanation of the concentration of Negro slaves there. It deserves mention that not all such substantial population centers were in fact coastal, though many were. Some few regimes of slave labor in the Northern colonies must indeed have turned a profit for traders and other canny enterprisers. Many did not, and that was especially true in the interior.

The economic justification of a slightly more extensive slave system was to be found in Pennsylvania, due both to larger farming enterprises and early industrial development. That the proportion of slaves was smaller than might have been expected is attributed by Phillips to two counterbalancing factors: the "disrelish" of slaveholding felt by many Quaker and German inhabitants, and the greater abundance of White immigrant labor. There were, however, some fairly large slaveholdings on country estates and in iron-works.[28]

EARLY ABOLITION IN THE NORTH

Despite the possible profitability of a small-scale slavery system in the North, slavery was either abolished or disappeared. Vermont inserted an anti-slavery provision in their constitution of 1777. In New Hampshire the system seems to have died out without express legal provision other than the inherent-liberty clause of the constitution. In Massachusetts, as already noted, a similar clause was the basis for abolition of slavery by court decisions of 1783 and 1785. Other Northern states provided for gradual abolition— Pennsylvania in 1780, Connecticut in 1784, Rhode Island in 1784, New York in 1788, and New Jersey in 1804. Part of these states later abolished the remnant of slavery outright, after the respective acts had been in force some years.[29]

The primary animus for the abolition of slavery in the North seems clearly to have been the liberal philosophy of the Revolutionary period. Two other factors, however, were associated with this ethical one: the value of slaves, even in the South, was during this period at a low level, for reasons to be discussed in a later chapter: and in the North slavery was opposed by free laborers.

That the existence of slavery was inconsistent with the doctrines of liberty, natural rights, and equality, as formulated in the
Declaration of Independence, occurred to some eloquent politicians, both North and South. The number of manumissions
increased in the South, and the way was open for Northern abolition. That this ethical sentiment was not alone responsible becomes clear when it is recognized that the sentiment was not a
sectional one. The question of numbers and economic importance
again is relevant. Whereas in the North slavery did not represent
a major economic investment and the number of prospective Negro
freemen raised few problems of subsequent racial relations, both
of these considerations were very important in the South. However,
the economic status of slavery in the South during and immediately following the Revolution led many Southern leaders, including Washington, Jefferson, Madison, and others, confidently to
expect its gradual decline and extinction.[30] The Northern states
could afford to be less cautious. But it is illogical for Arthur
Young Lloyd, a "Southern" historian, to reject ethical considerations on the part of early Northern abolitionists and manumit-
ters and accept such considerations on the part of Southerners.[31]
That kind of distortion of interpretation (U. B. Phillips was at
least as guilty) is the sort of nonsense that leads social scientists
properly to distrust historians. C. Vann Woodward, eminent historian of the South, takes such a seemingly dispassionate view of
American slavery and the disabilities placed on freed Negroes after
the Civil War as to become an apologist for the intrinsically wicked
system.[32]

Convincing evidence of an antipathy on the part of White laborers in the South to slavery comes from an outstanding states-
man of the period, John Adams. He wrote:

Argument might have [had] some weight in the abolition of slavery
in Massachusetts, but the real cause was the multiplication of labouring white people, who would no longer suffer the rich to employ these sable rivals so much to their injury . . . If the gentle-

men had been permitted by law to hold slaves, the common white people would have put the negroes to death, and their masters too, perhaps . . .

The common white people, or rather the labouring people, were the cause of rendering negroes unprofitable servants. Their scoffs and insults, their continual insinuations, filled the negroes with discontent, made them lazy, idle, proud, vicious, and at length wholly useless to their masters, to such a degree that the abolition of slavery became a measure of economy.[33]

The dearth of data concerning occupational distribution in the North and in the South is unfortunate. In none of the colonial enumerations nor in the Federal censuses before 1850, with one minor exception, was any occupational enumeration undertaken. The one exception was an enumeration of occupations of heads of families in Southwark and part of Philadelphia, Pennsylvania. The large proportion in manufacturing and mechanical pursuits (they were over two fifths)[34] suggests the possibility of a larger proportion of *free* laborers in the population of the North, particularly in urban centers, than in the South. Although free laborers were a much smaller proportion of the total urban and rural population of the North than were the slaves in the population of the South, they may well have carried a good deal more weight in the cities (where most of the slaves were held) than the few free laborers in the South.

That abolition in the North was not simply an automatic economic reaction on the part of slaveholders may be seen from two relevant facts: (1) there is slight, if any, evidence for a decline in the value of slavery, for the type of tasks performed, due to economic changes (though Southern markets were then depressed); (2) in no case, except possibly in New Hampshire, did slavery simply die out without legislative enactment; nor do the number of slaves at the time of abolition appear to have been smaller than at previous periods, except in those states which had previously provided by legislation for gradual abolition.

There is no evidence of widespread voluntary manumission of

slaves in the North before the legislative acts. It appears, rather, that the principal pressure for abolition came from non-slave-holders. True there may have been an element of political expedience among the slaveholders, for there were some realistic and expressed fears of arson and rebellion. Yet the number of slaves was small, held as individuals or as small groups, and "culturally assimilated." If the claim of John Adams be true, that the pressure came from White laborers, the reason for this antipathy to slavery will bear examination. One conceivable possibility is that the White laboring class felt a sort of class sympathy for the downtrodden Negro. This, however, squares neither with Adams' remarks nor with the subsequent failure to accept the free Negro on any terms of quality. A second possibility, suggested by Adams, is that slavery was interpreted as "unfair competition" in the labor market. Although there is little evidence of any oversupply of labor, this interpretation may still have been accepted. (A roughly comparable situation arose later in the South, when free White artisans in the larger towns and cities protested against the use of slave labor in their occupations. Moreover, the demeaning of occupations through their being performed by an inferior caste, particularly slaves, took otherwise honorable occupations out of the free labor market.)

An influx of immigration from Europe creating an oversupply of labor, one of the silly and tendentious arguments put forth by a Southern apologist such as Lloyd,[35] is simply not in accord with evidence readily available to him. (Lloyd deserves a fairly high position on the scale of irresponsibility reached by Southern historians. He suggests, for example, that Northern slaves were not freed but sold to the South. It may have happened, here and there, but census data give no confirmation.[36] Did he seek to make the sellers equally guilty with the buyers? And would that make the buyers one whit less guilty?) A fact, to which historians must attend if they are not to deserve the derogatory designation of *Southern* historians, is that immigration of White laborers across the Atlantic was practically at a standstill during the Revolutionary and immediate post-Revolutionary period. This was the period in which Northern abolition was accomplished or set in motion. Even in the period from 1790 to 1820 the United States Census estimates a total immigration of only 250,000. "Prior to 1820 there were very few immigrants; most of the number arriving prior to 1800 is so small as to be negligible." [37]

A third possible reason for the objection to slavery on the part of White laborers is the reflection that slavery may have produced upon the status of the laborer. Slavery was in obvious contradiction to the natural rights, inherent liberties, and equalitarian dogmas of the Revolution, which seemed to promise so much for the lower classes. If the contradiction were not self-evident, there was no dearth of popular literature, tracts calling it to public attention. Although there had been some anti-slavery literature, almost from the very beginning of the slavery system, its volume increased and its content was more vehement during this period. [38] Previously the arguments had largely been in terms of religious creeds and ethics; the arguments of the Revolutionary and early Federal periods were in terms of the philosophy of the Declaration of Independence. This propaganda had its effect, not only by showing that slavery was unjust in terms of this philosophy, but also that its continuance implied the possibility of further denials.

SLAVERY, NO; SLAVE-TRADE, YES

The inconsistency in the behavior of New England Yankees regarding slavery has been cited as demonstrating the insincerity of the ethical considerations in the abolition of slavery in the North. This inconsistency was the continued participation in the slave-trade by New England traders after domestic slavery had ceased to exist there. Participation in the slave-trade was in no New England state prohibited at the same time as domestic slavery was abolished. Most of these states did, however, legislate against such participation after some years. [39] These laws seem to have been poorly enforced, probably owing to the profits of the trade and certainly owing to the difficulty of prohibiting action that could only be effectively enforced outside the states concerned. It would be as ridiculous to suppose that the laws were not meant at all as to suppose that they were meant absolutely.

The importance of the slave trade in New England commerce has been testified to by a number of contemporaries.[40] In the type case it was part of a well-organized three-sided commerce. Molasses was brought from the West Indies to New England to be distilled into rum. The rum was taken to the African coast as payment for slaves, which in turn were brought to the West Indies or the coastal tobacco plantations. It was the second leg of this three-cornered trade, the transportation of Negroes across the Atlantic, which became famous or infamous, as the "Middle Passage." [41]

This trade came to the official attention of statesmen during the debates over the terms of agreement among the liberated but remarkably divergent American colonies. The Constitution provided for an end to the slave trade in 1808, this representing a difficult compromise. It can scarcely surprise us that just prior to the Constitutional deadline on the slave trade, the trade markedly increased.[42] The British shipowners carried their substantial share, as did shippers from both Northern and Southern states.[43] By country or region, no one was exempt from sin; unrecorded individuals may have been.

The participation of Yankee shippers in the slave-trade may be put down to sheer avarice, which we cannot discount. But the circumstance that slavery had become illegal in the North says something, though not much, about the collective view of human bondage in the North. Domestic bondage, White or Negro, slave or eventually-free, had been abolished. Trade had not and the enforcement of law outside domestic jurisdictions was out of the question. A man holding his servants in bondage was likely to come to public attention, because neighborhood gossips (out of envious malice, perhaps) would be likely to report him to local authorities. But if a captain loaded his ship with Negroes on the

West Coast of Africa for delivery at some Southern port, it might not come to official attention at all. Certainly the "fix" was in at the Southern ports, and that remained true until slavery was finally abolished after the Civil War. The venality of the slave-traders, Northern, Southern, or foreign, was only exceeded by the venality of the slave-importers. There were no sellers without buyers, and the buyers were Southern. Let no one mistake that. Without a demand, there would have been no supply.

Confronted with charges of the cruelty and immorality of the slave commerce, the traders defended the practice on a variety of grounds. These usually included the strictly commercial character of their activity, supplying the market for a legally recognized labor system in the South, and the local character of the moral judgments concerning slavery.[44] These defenses were, of course, rationalizations. But the very fact that it was thought necessary to rationalize, or explain away the inconsistency, is evidence of a value conflict. Two sets of values do not conflict when one is considered irrelevant or unimportant.

The argument here concerning the distinction between free labor in the North of the pre-Revolutionary American colonies and slave labor in the South has been cast mainly in economic terms. But since slave-holding was also, in all sections of the American wilderness, partly a matter of prestige and not profits, the prosperous Northerners were no more exempt from attempts at conspicuous display than were their Southern contemporaries. The facts are that abolition did take place in the North around the period of the American Revolution (give or take a couple of decades) and did not in the South. The economic interpretation of that difference is somewhat persuasive, but not totally so. Why would prosperous Northerners, if lacking any ethical compunctions, voluntarily give up the ownership of slaves? (To suppose that slave-holders were without political influence would be to indulge in wilful idiocy.) But lest morality be made to seem sectional, why would some prosperous slave-holders in the South conspicuously espouse abolition?

It is now popular to talk of costs and benefits, and that may help us here. But a bit of talk about timing may help, too. We shall return to the economics of slavery, but that later discussion does not bar a summary point or two here. At the time that the American labor systems got differentiated, North and South, the production of *goods* for the market was in the North still mainly in the hands of skilled artisans operating on a small scale. Otherwise, the North was specializing in trade and commerce, that is, *services* that at least required literacy for their performance and often considerable knowledge. Neither type of production was well suited to the use of slaves. In market terms, the production of goods, mainly in labor-intensive agricultural crops for export, was virtually all-important in the South. We could not let an economic interpretation stand alone, for no such view could ever hold, but we could not deny it a substantial relevance.

II

Industrialism and Wage Labor in the North

In the preceding chapter the labor system of the North and South was traced as it passed through a difference of degree to a difference of kind. Because of the small-scale farming and the trading, rather than industrial, economy in the North, the demand for labor was small throughout the colonial period. The availability of free or cheap land ruled out the economic possibility of wage labor, and two other sources supplied what labor deficiency existed: White indentured servants and Negro slaves. Bond servitude preceded slavery in both North and South, and in both sections slavery came to be introduced as a supplementary, rather than an alternative, system. The increasing importance of slavery, and its gradual supplanting of indentured servitude in the South have been noted, but slavery did not have a similar importance in the Northeast and ultimately, under economic and social conditions favorable to its abolition, gave way before an ethical opposition to it.

Thus one type of labor system, the type which had become characteristic in the South, ceased to exist in the North. The other principal labor system of the colonial period, White servitude, likewise ceased to exist, and about at the same time.

Because of the minor importance of *any* labor system other than independent artisans and family enterprises in the colonial North and in the absence of relevant statistical data, the relative importance of indentured servitude and slavery in the section is difficult to assess. What is more important for present purposes is the determination of how and why the former dilemma of White servitude or Negro slavery was ultimately avoided, and a free labor system established. As in any concrete historical case, a variety of factors were involved.

Although much of the preceding analysis of the labor system of the colonial North was in terms of conditions viewed as static, actually, of course, this was a conscious abstraction. Thus the availability of free or cheap land, and the consequent prohibitive wage scale of free laborers—who preferred independent enterprise—was posited as crucial in the establishment of the two types of bound labor. Now this condition during the course of the colonial period became decreasingly relevant; or, rather, decreasingly prevalent. For the frontier was ever farther from the seaboard ports and centers of population. Better lands during the later period were, short of an expensive trip to the unsettled West, already occupied. Under such conditions the advantage in occupying new, and possibly infertile, land was more questionable. Thus it follows that the statement that wage labor did not figure in the economic system of the North is ideal-typical for the period; it overlooks the dynamic aspect. There was *some* free labor before the disestablishment of slavery and indentured servitude. It may be, as Gray suggests,[1] that even during the colonial period, the Northern colonies received a greater number and proportion of prepaid (White) immigrants available, at least temporarily, for wage labor. It should also be noted that the supplanting of bound labor by free labor was in terms of labor systems, not of personnel. It was largely not a question of finding new wage laborers to replace bound servant and slave, but of simply changing the status of the unfree groups.

NORTHERN WHITE SERVITUDE: ABOLITION WITHOUT INTENT

The growth of the population, involving both its geographical expansion and urban concentration, provided a "permissive" condition for wage labor by reducing the possibility and advantage of individual enterprise. A number of other factors directly influenced the gradual extinction of White servitude. The Revolution necessitated an almost complete suspension of the servant trade for the duration of hostilities. England was opposed to the continued emigration of her subjects to an independent America. Transportation in English ships of persons for servitude for debt was prohibited in 1785, and the emigration of skilled workers was prohibited by Parliamentary acts of 1789 and 1794. In general, the necessity to migrate from Europe to escape religious persecution had been removed. At most, however, the importance of this factor was a possible change in the character of the migrants, since the number of immigrants increased from year to year. Social and economic conditions in Europe were better, and more immigrants were able to pay transportation. The voyage had become shorter and less expensive. American and European regulation of regulations of transportation decreased profit in the trade. Finally, as in the case of slavery, the Revolutionary philosophy was important. This exerted an informal and an indirect legal influence. "In the Middle and Northern States the system received its legal deathblow in the laws abolishing imprisonment for debt, because of the implied principle prohibiting control over freedom of the person." [2]

In no state was indentured servitude directly prohibited. Unlike slavery, the extinction of servitude took place automatically once it was assured that immigrants would not enter under indenture.

For White servitude could be maintained only by continual replacement; it lacked both the servitude for life and the self-perpetuation through the offspring, characteristic in the slavery regimes. The transition, moreover, required no change of attitude regarding the characteristics or rights of servants as persons. That is, all servants became freemen at the expiration of the term of servitude. Unlike slavery, servitude implied nothing as to the permanent status of the servant. Even in face of clear evidence to the contrary, as in the case of those unwillingly transported, the legal fiction of a contractual relationship was maintained. From the point of view of its legal sanction, the change to wage labor simply involved a change in the terms of the contract. Principally involved in the altered terms were the specified duration of the relationship, and a decreased control (but also decreased responsibility) on the part of the master-employer over the total activity of the servant-employee.

The Rise of Northern Manufacturing

The wage-labor system of the North, which before the Civil War was only slightly less "peculiar" to that section than slavery was to the South, was established *before* any large-scale labor system was required by the economic order. When industrial expansion (or the Industrial Revolution) began to move swiftly, the problem of the type of labor had already been settled.

Until early in the nineteenth century, economic activity north of Mason and Dixon's line had been primarily agricultural, secondarily commercial. Along the seaboard, however, where the large centers of population grew up, trading had been of increasing importance, both in statistical fact and in public policy. The latter is easily understood when it is realized that political leaders were typically drawn from the urban centers, the life of which depended upon trade. Thus it was that although a majority of the population in the North remained in agriculture until well into the nineteenth century, these colonies (later states) become known as trading and commercial regions. Prior to and during the war of 1812, however, trade and commerce were seriously curtailed, both by the uncertain character of sea trade, and, more particularly, by the American Embargo Act. Attention was shifted to manufacturing, especially to textile manufacturing, where the introduction of the power loom paved the way for a factory system. Adams writes:

New England textile mills which had been able to use only 500 bales of cotton in 1800 were calling for 90,000 by 1816, and the new industries, like snowballs rolling downhill, kept increasing their size with extra-ordinary rapidity. Between 1820 and 1831 in Massachusetts alone, the output of the cotton mills rose from $700,000 to $7,300,000, and of her woolens from $300,000 to $7,300,000.[3]

It would of course be quite erroneous to think of the establishment of an industrial economy as an immediate and clearcut break with the older order. Such a break is a long range effect. As Adams notes:

For the first two decades or more of the century, it was still an open question whether shipping or manufacturing was the most important New England industry, and as their interests were naturally opposed, there was confusion in political policies.[4]

As this same author notes elsewhere it was "not until the Tariff of 1828 that capital in New England had swung over to the factory from the ship to such an extent as to enable the manufacturer to outvote the merchant." [5]

The advent of industrial expansion in the North created a new condition, one which the South had known since early colonial times: the North needed a large and increasing labor supply. This demand was supplied in the first instance by former servants and slaves, and by the families of farmers in the rural areas surrounding the manufacturing towns. Although it was primarily the women and children of farm families who went to work in the cities, the more complete process of "urbanization" (at least in the spatial sense) was under way; indigent or struggling farmers on lands which, especially in New England, yielded small returns under the best of conditions, cast their lot with the new industrial order, but the local supply was inadequate, just as it always had been previously in the South. Immigration made up the deficiency.

IMMIGRANT LABOR WITHOUT INDENTURE

The estimated number of immigrants from 1790 to 1820 was only 250,000, or an annual average of 8,333.[6] After 1819, official reports on immigration were made through the State Department, and thus nearly accurate records are available. During the decade of the 1820's the annual average moved to 12,850 and then increased rapidly so that during the first half of the decade of the 1850's there were approximately 314,000 immigrants a year.[7]

Immigration was not, of course, confined *exclusively* to the North. Although the annual statistics are broken down by port of entry, this gives no reliable index of the subsequent residence of the immigrants, even as between the North and South, since the ports of New York and Boston had the lion's share of all sea-going trade. Not until 1850 did the United States census record the country of birth of the population, so that foreign-born population could be calculated, but the evidence there available confirms the universal agreement of authorities that migrants primarily settled in the Eastern and Middle states. Foreign-born population represented around 13 per cent in the Eastern states, 20 per cent in the Middle states, just over 5 per cent in the Southwestern states, and under 2 per cent in the Southern states.[8] These, it should be noted, are proportions of the *free* population. Had the computation been in terms of the total population, the percentages in the South and Southwest would be much less, due to the large number of slaves there.

It is of course an over-simplification of the situation to imply solely that Northern industry created a demand for labor, and that immigration supplied that demand. The expansion of Northern industry not only depended at least in part upon immigrant labor, but also tended to affect the supply. The latter is shown for example by the negative effects upon the number of immigrants following the crises of 1837 and 1857.[9]

But other factors were involved in determining the supply of White immigrants, particularly the potato famines in Ireland and Germany. Moreover, industrialism alone could not explain the differential proportion of immigrants in the North and South, since the South also had a labor deficiency. This is relevant to the adverse effect of slavery upon immigration, earlier noted, and discussed further in Chapter V.

Thus Northern industrial development, creating a labor demand larger than the natural increase of the population could supply, was aided by an influx of immigrant manual laborers, at times very nearly reaching the proportions of a mass exodus from some sections of Europe.

We reiterate that by the time that the North was on the road to the establishment of an industrial economy, dependent upon an increasing supply of cheap labor, the nature of the labor system had been established. The question of slave *versus* free labor was in the concrete circumstances meaningless. Comparisons might be made by economists, propagandists, or future thesis-writing doctorandi, but not as a meaningful problem by a Northern captain of industry. Slavery had been abolished, and the immigrants were at hand. No questions were necessary.

Wage Workers: Women and Children First

If no questions were necessary about the legal or institutional relationship of employer and employee, there was no dearth of problems arising in the concrete realm of social life. For what was in the course of establishment was an industrial capitalist economy, with a more or less permanent laboring class. And, as Adams has said, "There was little in common between the man who had and worked his own farm and the same man working on low wages for a mill owner in one of the new towns fast springing up." [10] And this difference in relation to the productive order remains of primary importance, over and above whatever similarities there may have been in "labor conditions," narrowly defined.

The hours of labor in growing Northern industries were, of course, long only by comparison with modern standards. The standard working day "from dark to dark" was not unusual for the time; the independent farmer found it necessary to work at least that long. The employment of women and children was likewise no basic departure from accepted practice on the small New England or Middle Atlantic farms. What was unusual, however, was the *disproportionate* employment of women and children. It was reported by a contemporary observer that of the six thousand persons employed in the cotton mills of Lowell, Massachusetts, in 1838, nearly five thousand were young women.[11] Schlesinger gives a more general description: "About sixty per cent of all the workers in the cotton mills of the Atlantic Seaboard from Virginia northward were women in 1831. Seven percent were children under twelve years of age." [12] Of the extent of employment of children, Craven gives additional evidence:

In 1820, children constituted 45 per cent of the cotton-mill labor in Massachusetts, 55 per cent in Rhode Island, and 54 per cent in Connecticut. Even in 1853, a commission in Rhode Island found 1,857 children under fifteen years at work from twelve to twelve and a half hours a day through eleven or twelve months of the year.[13]

The disproportionate number of women and children employed in the rising factories of the North was at least in part a concomitant of a basic economic transition. The appeal of steady, if meagre, wages was strong enough to lure those members of rural families who were least necessary in maintaining farm production. The factory provided a supplementary source of income, not only to bolster up the revenue from the scarcely profitable farm, but also, in the course of time, to purchase the products of the same or other factories. In this respect there was operating a special type of selective rural-urban migration: women and children first. As the transition to an industrial economy became more complete at least in the hinterland areas of the manufacturing cities and towns, the proportion. of women and children employed in the factories was partially reduced.

This interpretation is of course one-sided. It considers only the viewpoint of the prospective employee in terms of relative advantages in independent labor or factory employment. For many the "choice" was scarcely a real one; labor in the factory was an economic necessity. Moreover, the disproportionate employment of women and children depended on more than their greater availability; they were cheaper. Although able to tend the machines with as much efficiency as adult males, it was the consistent policy of employers to pay women and children less. Thus their employment was simply following a basic rule of industrialism, that of keeping labor costs at a minimum. However, it must be apparent that the availability of cheap labor and the cheapness of labor are in the concrete case reciprocal. This is simply an application of the economic principle that market price is determined by the intersecting of supply and demand curves.

Male farmers and those formerly self-employed as independent artisans came to the factories, either through choice or necessity. In some New England factories there came to be established a family-contract system of labor, whereby the whole family was employed as a unit, and the man with a large family had a competitive advantage in employment—not because of need, but because of the larger number of productive hands. Craven describes a Rhode Island situation:

The Rhode Island mill owners employed families as such, and fixed wages so that the earnings of all were necessary to keep the household going. Of a dozen families working for the Stater Company, 1817–19, and furnishing from three to seven children each, only two made enough to keep out of debt.[14]

Whatever the status in economics of the theory of a subsistence level of wages in a capitalistic economy, the practical application (perhaps unconscious) of the theory in the early period of American industrialism admits of little doubt. Indeed, I have generalized this interpretation:

The invariant and probably inevitable initial effect of industrialization is a polarization of social status *within the modernized sector.* The managers and the managed, the innovators and the reluctant followers, are likely to represent radical differences in education, income, and clearly, power.[15]

The Northern states represented a clear example of this principle early in the Nineteenth Century, and in fact a good deal later. A "laboring class," predominantly at a subsistence level, was established. During the ante bellum period there was, however, a notable change in the membership of this class. It was not only growing, but a disproportionate part of that growth was contributed by immigrants. This would have been true had no differential selective process been at work, since the labor demand increased at a rate greater than the natural increase of the population. But there did exist the additional process of "status succession": of filling in the lower positions in the economic order by new immigrants, while "Old Americans," and, later, older immigrants, moved up or out. Thus, "when native girls and families shook off rural standards and pressed for things which the new industrial life required they were quickly replaced with foreign workers whose dismal memories made acceptable all things American." [16]

FORMATION OF A WORKING CLASS

Adams noted that "By 1850 the good type of native New England men and women who had originally flocked to the mills to work had been driven out." [17] This is true, of course, only in relative terms. Although it is true that part of the "older stock" moved out —that is, emigrated to the West, there was by no means a complete shift in the type of labor personnel. What shift took place was by necessity, at this time, "up" before "out." That is, migration to the frontier required not only all the supposed virtues of the pioneers, but also an economic position better than that attained by the low-paid factory worker. Although the frontier has long been credited with relieving early hardship and tension in the industrial East, this safety-valve may be easily overrated. Schlesinger writes: "Individuals might escape the hardships of their class by moving to the frontier; but most of the wage-earners were discouraged from taking this step by large families, poverty, or lack of ambition. They were accordingly forced to work out their salvation at home." [18]

Orestes Brownson, an incisive contemporary observer, wrote in 1840: "Few, comparatively speaking, of the proletaries, in any of the old states, can ever become land-owners. Land there is already too high for that. The new lands are rapidly receding to the west, and can even now be reached only by those who have some little capital in advance." [19]

Had the "choice" between remaining an urban propertyless laborer and migrating to the frontier been a real one, there can be little doubt in which direction the decision would have been made. The best argument against ascribing too much importance to the possibility of escape to the frontier is the large numbers who did not escape. That the position of the urban worker in regard to migration was less advantageous than that of the independent farmer may be gathered from the fact that although by 1850 over

16 per cent of all persons born in the Eastern and Middle States had gone westward, nearly 27 per cent of those born in the Southern states had migrated.[20] Moreover, the misery, riots, and growth of a class-conscious labor movement in the industrial centers is ample evidence that the workers were forced to "work out their salvation at home."

Although reluctantly, laborers in the Northeast gradually acknowledged the existence of a class-structured society, and set about consolidating their interests. "Working Men's" parties were organized, first in Philadelphia in 1828, slightly later in New York and New England. Although short-lived, these political labor movements succeeded in obtaining more favorable legislation, and provided the groundwork for subsequent activity of a more purely economic sort, exemplified in the strike.[21]

At the same time that industrial labor was acting out an admission that economic democracy no longer existed, it was making vocal—and effective—demands for the extensions of political democracy. The Jeffersonian and Jacksonian periods are sometimes referred to by historians as the time of the "Rise of the Common Man." Although the "common man" was doing very little rising in the world of business and industry, he was making his weight felt in political affairs. During the early part of the Nineteenth Century there was a steady extension of the suffrage, chiefly through doing away with all or part of the property and similar restrictions. Although the movement was opposed by leading statesmen of the period, who looked with no favor upon the "unwashed masses," the political advantage entailed assured the outcome.[22]

Although this was the period of reform movements—many of them successful—and humanitarian legislation, the assumption must not be made that these did much for the "amelioration of the lot of the masses of mankind," or that the victories achieved were the result of the political dominance of labor, or its unbroken solidarity. Some progress toward a universal ten-hour day was made, mechanics' liens were allowed, and imprisonment for debt abolished. The propertyless character of the common laborer continued. Moreover, although the emphasis throughout the present chapter has been industrialization as a process moving toward completion, this was true only in the population centers of the seaboard.

The working class did not even provide a united front. The chief difficulty was the heterogeneity of its cultural background, due to the enormous influx of immigrants. Successive waves of immigrants tended to enter the industrial system at the bottom. This "status succession" was going on at the same time that native-born workers were coming to realize that independent economic activity, a definitely normative ideal in the Jefferson system, was giving way before the Industrial Revolution. Adams makes the perceptive observation with respect to the attitudes of American workers toward immigrants that "the contempt for the foreigner began to be transferred to the work he did," and specifically compares this with the attitudes of Southern free workers toward the work done by Negro slaves.[23] Industrial unrest, and the language and religious differences of the immigrants, provided the basis for a "nativist" or chauvinistic reaction in the midst of the reforms. This was exemplified in the "Know-Nothing" party (officially, the American Party) which carried some political influence in the last decade before the Civil War. Although in a sense a countermovement to the political tendencies of the times, it points as clearly as the strikes, riots, and political clamors to the almost complete dependence of the worker upon holding his job. Thus, when wages, and even jobs, were threatened by a mass of immigrant laborers, an antiforeign movement arose in an attempt not only to limit the labor supply, but also to prevent the newcomers from exercising the political prerogatives of "100 per cent Americans." If this straw seemed to be blowing in a different direction from the others, it was blown by the same wind.

Perhaps the dynamic character of social relationships in the North from roughly 1790 to 1860 may be summarized in the statement that there developed an increasing discrepancy between political and economic democracy. In the decades prior to the Civil War, there had developed in the North an increase in political democracy, at least as measured by the extension of the suffrage. But from an economic situation where each bread-winner was typically independent there had developed a class-structured industrial hierarchy. Whatever previous class distinctions had existed —and they were definitely present—these distinctions did not rest primarily on differences in relations to the "means and instruments of production." Property had previously meant property in land, and the property owned by the least prosperous was different from that owned by the "gentry" only in quantity. But the Industrial Revolution brought a more definite division between the capitalist —who owned capital goods, or papers representing capital goods —and the laborer, who "owned" (in distinction from the slave) his own labor.

That no amount of political democracy could have brought a return to the older economy of small farmers and independent artisans needs only the demonstration of subsequent history. In fact, it is possible that the diversion of attention and energy to the political field retarded the development of an economically powerful labor movement. But whatever the economic disadvantages of Northern laborers, even in comparison with slave labor—a favorite comparison of pro-slavery spokesmen, to be discussed later—this was a system of "free" labor. There were no *official* restraints upon a laborer becoming a capitalist. The "log-cabin to President" or "ditch-digger to Capitalist" ideology was already in force. It was against an economic background such as this that the reform demanded by an ethical valuation of the individual was attempted. It was out of a situation of manhood suffrage and "wage slavery" that the abolitionists decried the evils of the official slavery in the South.

III

The Economics
of Slavery

If we compare the intersection of ethics and economics with respect to labor systems in the American colonies (and subsequent states), North and South, the ethics seem to be a bit skimpy on either side. We have traced the early differentiation of labor systems, the relatively early abolition of slavery in the North (with some more-than-slight deference to ethical compunctions), and the subsequent development of a free but exploitive labor system in the North. Slavery had a different fate in the South.

Unlike the relatively undeveloped slave labor system in the North, the South fitted slavery, from its very inception, into the plantation system of colonial management. Thus until about 1790 the extension of slavery in the South was about co-terminus with the extension of tobacco, rice, and indigo plantations. The tobacco plantations formed the basic economic life of Virginia and Maryland, and later extended into North Carolina. Rice and indigo cultivation was confined to the swampy coasts of South Carolina and Georgia. We are not engaged in an economic history of Southern commercial agriculture, but it is necessary to examine briefly the status of the slave-plantation economy during its "critical period" —roughly, from the Revolution until around 1820.

During the Revolution, tobacco exports as well as those of rice and indigo, fell sharply. Whereas in the case of tobacco the volume of exports was largely regained in the decade following the close of war, resulting from an expansion of the tobacco-growing area to the south and west; indigo, which had been cultivated under special British subsidies for naval uses, practically ceased to exist as a commercial crop. Rice, however, remained of large commercial importance along the South Atlantic coast, and helped maintain a demand for slave labor in the region.[1]

ECONOMIC PROBLEMS OF TOBACCO GROWING

Quite apart from the influence of trade difficulties during the hostilities, the old and populous tobacco region, which had been the principal mainstay of the plantation-slavery system, had for some years been running into difficulties. Chief among them was the problem of soil exhaustion. The constant "cropping" of tobacco caused a continued decline in the size and quality of crops. Thoughout the old tobacco-growing areas there was an increasing shift to raising cereals and to general farming. This left the large Virginia and Maryland slaveholders with an extra labor supply.[2] (Soil exhaustion is of course relative to the current state of technical agricultural practices, including use of natural and artificial fertilizers. Tobacco, however, is a crop more demanding than most on the unaided natural fertility of soils. A substantial portion of the yield was sold in tobacco leaf, and there is no assurance that even commercially unusable stems were returned to the soil; so tobacco farmers were in effect strip mining the earth.)

The situation in the old tobacco belt was one of the chief factors in the "critical period" in slavery during the years following the Revolution. Several other changes had been going on during the period. There had been a migration of Northern and European farmers into the back country of the South.

From about 1775 to 1790 the population of Virginia increased from 420,000 to 747,610, in spite of the fact that large numbers were moving from Virginia into the sparsely settled back parts of the Carolinas and Georgia, and new lands made available by Indian cessions, and into Kentucky and Tennessee.

This extensive migration of white farmers reduced the numerical weight and economic and political influence of the slaveholding population.[3]

Furthermore, the artisan class in the South had been made prosperous during the war, and exerted its influence against any employment of slaves in nonagricultural occupations.[4]

The "Critical Period" in Slavery

To the aforementioned factors must be added the ethical opposition to slavery arising out of the Revolutionary philosophy. This ethical opposition was certainly as strong in the South as in the North. Washington, Jefferson, Madison, and many other Southern leaders represented not only the serious economic straits of slaveholders, but also the opposition to a continuance of slavery. Many of their statements regarding slavery were later quoted to Southerners by Abolitionists.[5]

This "critical period" did not prevail in Georgia and South Carolina and although indigo practically disappeared as a commercial crop, rice culture continued unabated thereby insuring a continued demand for slave labor along the swampy coastal lands. There is little evidence that the continuance of slavery in this region was ever seriously questioned. It was also in this area that sea-island cotton was introduced, and that proved decisive.

Elsewhere, however, the question of the future status of slavery was seriously contested. The gradual abolition of slavery was seriously debated in the border states, losing only by a narrow margin. These states preceded the Federal government in the prohibition of slave importations. Manumissions in Delaware, Maryland, and Virgina increased enormously. In Virginia, for example, there were in 1782 less than 2000 free Negroes, while there were 12,866 in 1790, 20,124 in 1800 and 30,750 in 1810.[6] Prices for slaves saw a marked decline.[7]

Although Georgia and South Carolina are not to be included in the areas affected by a declining economic justification for slavery, the distribution of slaves was such that this limitation on the general characterization of this period as "critical" is of less importance than it might otherwise appear. The first Federal census of 1790 revealed that around four-fifths (79.3 per cent) of the total Southern slave population was then located in the "border states" (Delaware, Maryland, Virginia, North Carolina, Kentucky, and "Southeast Territory,"—which became Tennessee). Over two-fifths of that population (44.5 per cent) was in Virginia alone.[8] Thus, most of the slave system in the South at the beginning of the Nineteenth Century was subject to the adverse economic conditions just noted.

We have already noted that sentiment against slavery failed to have the same strength and result in the South as in the North primarily resulting from a difference in the concrete situation. Despite the real economic difficulties of the slavery system in the border states, the sheer numbers of the Negroes and the amount of capital invested in them as property assured effective resistance to immediate abolition. The general feeling seems to have been that legally imposed gradual abolition was unnecessary, since the economic difficulties of the times pointed to this eventuality through the continuation of economic interests.

The situation, then, in the last years of the Eighteenth Century and the first years of the Nineteenth Century was of a well-established system of slave labor, used in plantation agriculture, and largely bound to the fate of commercial plantation crops. Commercial plantation crops depended, of course, on suitable, available soil, and this imposed limitations upon expansion of the slave plantations. Expansion was necessary since productivity of much of the soil on the seaboard had been exhausted—at least so far as profitable, one-crop farming without fertilizer was concerned. Commercial agriculture with slave labor had come to a "critical period."

Had there been no new crop, no new technology, and no new land resources, slavery might well have come to an end as a *labor system* in the South (though perhaps surviving as a status symbol among the wealthy). Upland cotton made the crucial difference, fitting the geographical, technological, economic and social needs of the declining region.

COTTON BECOMES KING

Cotton had been grown in the South on a small scale for domestic use since the early days of American colonization. It had not developed into a genuinely commercial crop for several reasons. Chief among these was the absence of any large market for the product. Domestic manufacture was consistently prohibited by English authorities, and the demand in England remained small as long as hand spinning and weaving persisted.

The great difficulty of cleaning seeds and impurities from the fiber proved a second deterrent to the commercial growing of cotton. This meant that the labor cost was almost prohibitively high.

Three distinct changes in the situation paved the way for cotton to become the major commercial crop of the South.

The first of these chronologically, and perhaps in basic importance, was the invention and introduction of textile manufacturing machinery in England as an aspect of the Industrial Revolution. These inventions came at about the time of the American Revolution and provided the technological base for an effective market demand for cotton.

The second change was the introduction of a new variety of cotton with seeds which could easily be removed with a simple "roller gin." This Bahama or sea-island cotton could be grown, however, as the name implies, only along the south Atlantic coast and the islands off-shore. Its principal effect, therefore, was to provide a substitute for the declining indigo industry. However, this long-staple cotton commanded the highest price on the market, and its production rapidly increased, as shown by the volume of exports from South Carolina, which rose from under 10 thousand pounds in 1789 to over 8 million pounds in 1801.[9]

The invention of the "saw gin" by Eli Whitney in 1793 removed the geographical limitations on the commercial growing of cotton. The gin mechnically removed the seeds from the short-staple upland cotton. Whereas one person could prepare about one pound of lint a day by hand labor, the first gin could comb about fifty pounds. Further technical improvements greatly increased the output of the machine and far surpassed that original figure. The cotton gin had an immediate effect reflected both in increased production and geographical expansion of the productive area. The crop of 1794 was estimated at 8 million pounds, a large part of which was sea-island cotton. This figure was doubled by 1798, and in 1864 the estimated crop was over 64 million pounds. From the seaboard the cotton producing area quickly spread to the Piedmont, and later into the Mississippi basin.

There remained, of course, geographical limitations to the profitable operation of the plantation-slavery system for cotton production. After the problem of market accessability had been solved by improved transportation facilities, there still remained areas in which, for reasons of climate or soil, cotton could not profitably be grown. This was true to a limited degree in the absolute sense, but more particularly as related to two economic variables: cost of slaves and price of cotton. Slave prices began to spiral while cotton prices fell, which meant that some areas—soil fertility remaining constant—which formerly yielded a margin of profit became submarginal, at least for cotton culture. Even more important were the areas in which fertility did not remain constant, and were abandoned, to cotton cultivation, in favor of new land. Cotton growers were given to soil "mining" as were the tobacco growers, though possibly at a slower rate and through no virtue of their own.

Variations in specific geographical conditions throughout the South were, therefore, relevant to the establishment and expansion of the particular economic configuration which came to characterize (at least symbolically) the entire South—*given* a market demand for the product, a labor system (slavery) and a method of commercial agriculture (plantation system).

THE PLANTATION SYSTEM

Certainly slavery and the plantation system were not present in equal degree or kind throughout the South. It follows that although it is perfectly legitimate to speak of the "South" as a unit, or ideal-typical configuration of relationships, there were substantial differences in both time and space. Thus our description of the plantation method of agricultural production, and its relation to a system of capitalized labor, will involve both a cross-sectional description of the ideal-typical organization, and some attention to the significant spatial and temporal variations.

Gray has given a formal definition and explanation of the plantation system:

The plantation was a capitalistic type of agricultural organization in which a considerable number of unfree laborers were employed under unified direction and control in the production of a staple crop. The definition applies to the South, however, only in the ante bellum period, for plantation organization has prevailed since the Civil War on the basis of labor that is at least nominally free. The definition implies also that (1) the functions of laborer and employer were sharply distinct; (2) the system was based on commercial agriculture, except in periods of depression; (3) the system represented a capitalistic stage of agriculture development, since the value of slaves, land, and equipment necessitated the investment of money capital often of a large amount and frequently borrowed, and there was a strong tendency for the planter to assume the attitude of the business man in testing success by ratio of net money income to capital invested; and (4) there was a strong tendency toward specialization—the production of a single crop for market.[10]

It is perhaps more confusing than helpful to refer to plantation systems of agricultural production as "capitalistic." That the landowner wished to exploit his workers or tenants and live well cannot be denied. But that did not distinguish him from a feudal landlord. In fact, in contemporary Latin America, the hacienda, fazenda, latifundia, or estancia represents a comparable agricultural organization. Most of the examples represent situations in which the actual laborers are not totally free (for example, serfdom or peonage or *enquilaje*), but truly capitalistic rationality is commonly impaired by an over-abundance of subordinates. Thus some labor represented, in effect, consumer goods and not capital goods.

The capitalization of labor, through slavery, was not a truly essential feature of the plantation system. It was, perhaps, more forthright if not more commendable than the other forms of un~~freedom that plantation owners and managers have exploited~~. But with true capitalization, the labor force represented in the South perhaps the major investment—as compared to land, buildings, and equipment. Land prices varied, of course, according to quality and location, but were never very high, due to the continued availability throughout the ante bellum period of cheap lands on the receding frontiers. The existence of cheap lands undoubtedly explains, on the economic level, the failure of land prices to fluctuate materially with variations in the market price of the staples produced. Typically, however, land was not a once-and-for-all investment, but had to be recapitalized, ordinarily in the form of new land, about every twenty years. This is a rough average, since the "period of grace" for new lands before soil exhaustion depended on type of soil, the staple grown, and to a certain extent, on efficiency of management. The circumstance that much of Southern commercial agriculture resembled the shifting agriculture repeatedly reinvented in tropical rain forests seems not to have come to the attention of comparative anthropologists or comparative economists.

On a proper plantation, buildings included the owner's "big house," an overseer's house (or cabin), cabins for the laborers (slaves), and a wide variety of sheds, stables, barns, and other outhouses. All buildings with the exception of the main house, and often even that, were of inexpensive construction. The relative frequency of moving kept investment in construction at a minimum, consistent with reasonable efficiency, and, perhaps, comfort. Tools and equipment were largely simple and inexpensive, especially on the cotton plantations. The most expensive equipment was required for sugar plantations, which required investments of a permanent nature and were not subject to such high depreciation costs. Farm animals varied in number and kind, but usually included horses, mules, and often pigs and cows.

In addition to labor costs, running expenses on plantations included taxes, equipment and stock upkeep, and, very important though seldom precisely computed, interest and depreciation. Exact cost accounting was almost unknown in the pre-war plantation system. That this was not more frequently disastrous was no doubt due to the fact that the plantation system was combined with slavery, so that a major portion of the capitalization was in the labor supply, a fairly fluid investment. Slaves were bought, and, occasionally, sold, as prosperity or depression was the lot of the planter.

Let us take as an ideal-typical example a large and nominally fully commercial plantation. (That is, we are avoiding the almost totally spurious, Virginia-based, stereotype of a pleasant, feudal relation between the master and his faithful servants: "darkies" strumming banjos in the evening under the magnolia trees.) Whether the large, commercial plantation had a resident or an absentee owner, immediate management was under the direction of the overseer. He had the dual responsibility of handling the labor force, and, in order to keep his position, of producing a large crop. Since the criterion of the crop was crucial, and at any time the capitalized labor was a "given," there was strong pressure on the overseer to overwork labor. (Never mind nice, humanitarian grounds. If labor is capitalized, as in slavery, short-term exploitation—read rationality—may lead to long-term irrationality —read idiocy. That was typical of the economics of the plantation economy.)

Various gangs of the labor force were under the immediate supervision of "drivers" or foremen, selected from the ranks of the slaves. Relatively high efficiency was insured by a definite, and rather elaborate, schedule of regulations for both overseer and laborer. These included rules for regular inspection by the overseer; hours of rising, eating meals, quitting work, and going to bed; quantity and type of clothing and food, and how apportioned; necessary rest; division and apportionment of labor; and necessary supervision and punishment.

As the system became increasingly rationalized, planters of a literary or at least managerial and communicative bent, found ways of communicating their advanced thoughts on slave management. *De Bow's Review* was a favorite periodical for the dispassionate, rational-management set of slaveholders. Some, it is true, hid behind pseudonyms or descriptive aponyms, but others signed themselves with their own names, as if with true dignity, as if with honor. "Agricola," "Mississippi Planter," and "Small Farmer" were properly integrated with John A. Calhoun, St. George Cocke, and Robert Collins.[11]

For his captive laborers, the commercial slaveholder provided rude houses, usually log cabins, one for each "family." (We shall later note that families were not at all alien to African culture, but that slave families in the American sense often constituted rather casual arrangements, both on the part of participants and particularly on the part of market-oriented slaveholders.) The slave cabin was a one room affair, furnished with crude furniture and some type of bedding. It is difficult to determine the usual size of these on the large plantations, except in terms of the maximum. Those interested in managerial efficiency urged "ample" housing space. Typical of these was the writer who insisted that self-interest was on the side of humanity. "A negro house," he wrote, "should never be crowded. One sixteen or eighteen feet square is not too large for a man and woman and three or four small children." [12]

Clothing was generally issued at regular intervals, usually twice a year. It was rough and serviceable, but, critics claimed, inadequate. The following statement of clothing allowances may be taken as typical:

Hammond's clothing allowance was for each man in the fall two cotton shirts, a pair of woolen pants and a woolen jacket, and in the spring two cotton shirts and two pairs of cotton pants, with privilege of substitution when desired; for each woman six yards of woolen cloth and six yards of cotton cloth in the fall, six yards of light and six of heavy cotton cloth in the spring, with needles, thread and buttons on each occasion. Each worker was to have a pair of stout shoes in the fall, and a heavy blanket every third year. Children's cloth allowances were proportionate and their mothers were required to dress them in clean clothes twice a week.[13]

Food was likewise rationed out on a bi-weekly basis. Meal and salt or fresh meat were the staples, with sugar, molasses, coffee, and flour as occasional "luxuries." [14] The unit of distribution was the food for a week for one "hand" (young adult male field hand in good physical condition). Women, children, house servants, the aged and infirm were given food allowances according to their fractional rating in terms of this unit. Thus women who worked in the fields and house servants might be counted as "three-quarter hands," children as "half-hands," and so forth. This rating, it will be observed later, was also resorted to in the assignment of tasks or division into gangs.

Because of the diversity of practice in regard to the extent of plantation self-sufficiency, food and clothing expenses are difficult to determine. The large commercial plantation, however, reduced self-sufficiency to a minimum, devoting almost exclusive attention to the production of the staple crop for market. This was particularly true in the less isolated regions. Supplementary and maintenance crops were probably the rule, however, rather than the exception.

Estimates of annual expenses are available, and though varying somewhat, are uniformly low. Money expenses on smaller, less specialized establishments, were still lower. "The highest contemporary estimate, made by a State engineer of Louisiana, was $72.60 per head. This represents the purchase cost of all items of food, clothing, shelter, and medical attendance for 103 slaves owned and employed by the State of Louisiana." [15] Since it may be assumed that all, or nearly all, of these slaves were able-bodied males or the equivalent of "prime field hands," the ordinary ratio on the plantation of one "hand" to two slaves would mean that the estimate could be cut in half for a normal age-sex distribution. This would considerably reduce its departure from other estimates. For a large cotton plantation, budget estimates include the following: [16]

To feed 100 servants, to furnish the hospital, overseer's table &c	$750
To clothe 100 slaves, shoe them, furnish bedding, sacks for gathering cotton &c	750
Wages to competent overseer	700
Medicine, doctors' bills, &c	250

Omitting the overseer's wages, the annual budget would be $1750 or $17.50 per laborer. It is interesting that the wages of the overseer, whose occupation was certainly not regarded as a highly paid or honorable one, amounted to almost half as much (47 per cent) as the expenses of 100 slave laborers. How much of this low-cost maintenance of a plantation labor supply should be attributed to the fact that it was a *slave* labor force is difficult to determine. Certainly under a system of capitalized labor, interest and "depreciation" (or replacement) might be added to labor expenses. But the low cost points to a great deal of industrial or commercial efficiency of the plantation system itself.

The management and direction of labor was vital on the plantation. The primary division of labor was between house and field servants. Field servants, divided into gangs, performed various tasks, or, at times, the same tasks at different rates of speed. The amount and type of work for any gang was determined primarily by how its members were rated according to the classifications: "hands," "three-quarters basis," or some other fraction. It was important for economy of supervision to reduce disparity of strength or ability within any gang to a minimum. There were in addition a large number of artisans and functionaries, such as blacksmiths, carpenters, coopers, millers, boatmen, and generally one steward. Small gangs or special tasks were designed for children, aged persons, and the partially incapacitated. It was a primary requirement of the plantation system, whether using slave labor or not, that every person in the force contribute something to the productivity of the establishment. What slavery added to the plantation system was a difference in the degree of stringency of regulation, plus a nearly absolute control over rewards and punishments. The plantation system and slavery are not to be confused, but they were in fact linked in the ante bellum American South.

COMMERCIAL AGRICULTURE:
EARLY JUSTIFICATIONS OF SLAVERY

The method of capitalizing and maintaining the commercial agricultural organization of the South was primarily that of a credit system. Although it is difficult to see any necessary or inherent relationship of a plantation system to a credit economy, the two were from the beginning historically linked in America. In the colonial period credit was required to establish capitalistic agriculture chiefly for want of local capital. Gray notes that in the colonial period, "The credit system frequently made the planter an economic vassal of the merchant. Not infrequently accounts between merchants and planters ran for years without being balanced." [17] This situation continued during the entire period of the developed plantation and slavery systems. It seems to have been a concomitant of the highly competitive nature of plantation agriculture, requiring constant expansion to increase efficiency. Expansion entailed new capital investments, ordinarily made in the first instance with borrowed money. The common source from which money was borrowed was the merchant or factor. The latter might be a "Yankee," or himself in turn dependent upon Northern bankers. It was a frequent complaint of Southern planters that Northern bankers reaped more profit from the plantation-slavery organization than did the Southern planters themselves. Although slaves sometimes provided the security for credit advancements, the typical arrangement was a contractual or unofficial lien upon the forthcoming crop.[18] The credit arrangement was particularly significant in that it gave added weight to the persistence of the typical plantation one-crop system. The planter, in debt for equipment, supplies, or capitalized labor, had to keep planting the crop which would yield the surest *monetary* return in a regular commercial market. The influence was, however, undoubtedly reciprocal. The one-crop plan of plantation agriculture, by reducing the extent of self-sufficiency to a minimum, placed the planter in a money economy, in which he was almost completely dependent even for food and clothing upon cash in hand or credit to be secured. Eventually, he was dependent upon a good crop at an adequate price; failing one or the other, one either borrowed on the future, or sacrificed capital investments already made.

An inevitable consequence of agriculture so completely commercialized and so dependent upon a well-developed credit system was a tendency to speculation. But that tendency often served to put commercial money-lenders in charge of productive properties, and that is a tale that has since been told wherever commercial agriculture has appeared.

The term "monoculture" was, I believe, introduced since the original version of this study was completed. But that is unimportant. Gray, who to date is one of the few sensible commentators on the economics of slavery in America,[19] thinks that addiction to cotton-growing or tobacco-growing (in the older pattern of slavery) on the part of planters was a combined product of geography and climate, on the one hand, and economic and social organization, on the other. Marketing mechanisms, the experience and knowledge of the planter, his overseer, and his slaves were all fitted to a monoculture system of commerical agriculture; not to diversification or crop rotation.

These features of the plantation system of agricultural production are important not only to the understanding of the organizational features of slavery in the South, but also in the analysis of the dynamics of that organization which the combination of the features of a plantation economy with slave labor produced.

The description of the plantation system, with its large labor force working under close supervision at largely non-technical or semi-technical tasks, already partially implies its adaptability to the use of slave labor. The basis for the union of the plantation system with slave labor may perhaps be shown with greater distinctness if the problem is approached from the other side: what conditions were essential to a profitable large-scale slavery system?

THE PROFITABLE USE OF SLAVES

Plantation systems can exist without peonage or slavery. And slavery can exist without plantation agriculture: as domestic servants, as forms of sexual exploitation, as conspicuous display of power and affluence, as servants of the state in various public works. Yet for the *commercial* exploitation of capitalized labor, the plantation offers a number of distinctive features. (Here we are especially indebted to Hammond, who made the equation of plantations and slavery too constrictive, on both sides.[20]) (1) The plantation required a large number of simple, repetitive tasks. The slave was neither trained nor motivated for more complex assignments. For such tasks all ages and sexes may be used, save only infants and the extremely ill or infirm. (2) A long growing season and ample off-season tasks help keep the labor force fairly steadily employed. (3) Means of subsistence (whether locally produced on the plantation or bought) need to be cheap. (4) Large-scale organization of labor permits reduction of the relative costs of supervision. Hammond argues from these and similar considerations that cotton was an ideal plantation crop for a slave labor system. It is fairly labor-intensive (before mechanization), and even has the advantage (as, say, compared with mature maize) that the plants are low enough that workers can be seen and thus subject to constant surveillance.

The first condition, simplicity of labor, is apparently an essential one for the profitable large-scale use of slave labor, not because of any inherent inferiority of the Negro, but because of the fact of slavery itself. Slave labor required close supervision because it was forced labor, and extensive division of labor and perfection of special techniques would unduly magnify the problem of supervision. Moreover, it is true that slavery put some limits to the learning of technical skills through the inadequate instruction provided. There was a constant pressure to forego a possible increase in future productivity in favor of early incorporation of children into gangs for the production of the staple crop.

The requirement of simplicity of labor does not rest upon any inferiority of the slave laborer as a person. Aside from a long line of "fire eaters" and other pro-slavery apologists, perhaps U. B. Phillips has been the greatest offender in this type of interpretation. Because of Phillips' position as a specialist in the history and interpretation of American slavery and the persistence of this type of interpretation, it merits some consideration. In his chief work

Phillips writes: "On the whole the plantations were the best schools yet invented for the mass training of that sort of inert and backward people which the bulk of the American Negroes represented." [21] In various special articles he makes his position more abundantly clear.

Negro slave labor was expensive, not so much because it was unwilling as because it was overcapitalized and inelastic. The Negro of himself, by reason of his inherited ineptitude, was inefficient as a self-directing laborer in civilized industry. . . .
A slave among the Greeks or Romans was generally a relatively civilized person, whose voluntary labor would have been far more productive than his labor under compulsion. But the Negro slave was a Negro first, last and always, and a slave incidentally. [22]
. . . The plantation system was probably the most efficient method ever devised for the use of stupid labor in agriculture on a large scale. [23]

Quite apart from any anthropological evidence, which Phillips apparently thinks it unnecessary to adduce, this type of interpretation is on very shaky ground historically. Although it is true that the large bulk of plantation labor was unskilled labor, some artisans and workers with technical skills were necessary; these were almost uniformly recruited from among the slaves. A large labor force working at various diversified skilled tasks could not be instituted with slave labor, not because of lack of resources in ability, but because under forced labor the supervision and direction of such work would be impossible on a large scale. That the capacities of Negroes to become skilled workers were recognized at the time is shown not only by their presence in some numbers among town slaves—reported incidentally by Phillips[24]—but also by a series of protests from White laborers against employment of slaves in technical and non-agricultural occupations. [25]
    The claim that large-scale slavery was necessarily limited to agricultural labor will also warrant closer examination. In the first place, it is not at all clear that the factory system, with routinized labor, with technical skills reduced to a minimum through the use

of automatic machinery, involves a requirment of particularly greater skill than does agricultural labor. Although Phillips at one place claims, "This peculiar labor system failed to gain strength in the North, because there was no work which negro slaves could perform with notable profit to their masters," [26] at another place he admits ". . . just as in the case of the factory system, which of course is entirely analogous as regards labor organization, the success of [the plantation] industry depended upon its regularity and the constant repetition of similar tasks." [27]

Most convincing, however, is the historical evidence of the successful employment of slave labor in manufacturing and construction work. Gray reports:

. . . in the case of several important industries the assumption that Negro slaves were incapable of effective employment was disproved. A number of cotton factories were operated in whole or in part by slave labor, and it was found that slaves were capable of performing effectively many of the simpler routine operations. On the Cumberland river, in Tennessee, nearly 60 per cent of the laborers in the iron industry were slaves, and they were employed elsewhere for coal mining. In 1842 slave labor was introduced in the Tredegar iron works at Richmond, Virginia, as an experiment. They were so successfully trained in the processes of puddling, beating, and rolling that after 1845 they constituted the majority of the operatives. In the lumbering industry in North Carolina slave labor was very profitable. Slaves were successfully employed in mining, quarrying, canal-building, and railway construction, in which lines of employment contractors frequently preferred slave labor. In Georgia more than 1,000 miles of railroad were constructed by slaves, and in North Carolina 223 miles.[28]

So far, then, as simplicity of labor and ease of direction are concerned, it may be concluded that these were conditions necessary to the large-scale use of slave labor. These conditions the plantation method of agricultural production met, but so did the factory system. That the combination of slave labor with factory production was of slight importance in the South, and non-existent in the North, is therefore to be explained by factors other than the incompatibility of the two systems.

Slavery introduced a complicating factor into the classical trichotomy of land, labor, and capital. The cost of slave labor was both a capital and a labor expense. From what one may call the "traditional" economic view, as ably expressed by Phillips, this amounted to an added cost of slave labor.

An expert accountant [Arthur R. Gibson, *Human Economics* (London, 1909), p. 202] has well defined the property of the master in his slave as an annuity extending throughout the slave's working life and amounting to the annual surplus which the labor of the slave produced over and above and cost of his maintenance. Before any profit accrued to the master in any year, however, variouns deductions had to be subtracted from this surplus. These included interest on the slave's cost, regardless of whether he had been reared by his owner or had been bought for a price; amortization of the capital investment; insurance against the slave's premature death or disability and against his escape from service; insurance also for his support when incapacitated whether by illness, accident or old age; taxes; and wages of superintendence. None of these charges would any sound method of accounting permit the master to escape.[29]

However, as Gray points out that ". . . the question of the relative competitive advantages of slave labor and of free labor was confused from time to time by a tendency to assume that the interest and replacement fund calculated at a certain rate on the capital value of the slave was an extra cost which the employer of free labor did not have to assume, representing therefore a special and notable disadvantage in the case of slave labor. Such an assumption, however, was the reflection of incorrect economic analysis. When capitalization was accurately effected, the series of successive incomes as they become available actually were equivalent to interest and replacement; for interest and replacement would have been allowed for in the relatively low value that the owner paid for the services of the slave, capitalized on a terminable basis. In short, the process of capitalization obscures the fact that the so-called interest on investment and the replacement fund constitute actually the surplus over cost of maintenance appropriable from the ownership of the slave." [30]

The capitalization of labor, aside from the problems of accountancy raised, did tend to cut down economic elasticity and versatility through fixing labor in one line of employment. In conjunction with all the other forces toward continued one-crop commercialism, such as the credit system, competitive specialization, and dependence upon the money economy, the capitalization of labor represented such a major investment that experimentation in non-commercial crops or in untried market products was fairly well discouraged.

SLAVERY AS A WELFARE SYSTEM

As often pointed out by pro-slavery writers, and insisted upon by some later historians, the slave had (at least in theory) some advantages over the free laborer by reason of his ownership. The slave, representing a long-time investment, was protected, the argument runs, from ruthless exploitation and subsequent discard. It was to the owner's self-interest to keep his working force at top productive capacity for the longest possible period of time. The slave was cared for in time of sickness, and possibly in old age. Had every planter figured his costs and advantages with great precision, the care of the temporarily incapacitated worker would be sensible, and the care of the clearly and permanently incapable would make no sense at all. The absence of careful calculation often worked to the productive slave's disadvantage, and to the advantage of other charges upon the slaveholders' slight sense of humanity. The continual and immediate pressure for money from the sale of a good crop, the policy of judging overseers in terms of the size of the crop, and the general absence of cost accounting inevitably created pressure to disregard long-term returns on capital invested in slaves in favor of immediate profits. Although there is little evidence of a *deliberate* "working slaves to death" and replacing them more often, there is ample evidence that planters, and especially overseers, were prone to overlook the full implications of capitalized labor and adopt a practice of immediate exploitation.[31]

Economic Advantages of Slave and Free Labor

The question of the relative economic advantages of slave and free labor was debated with some heat and not much enlightenment during the existence of the slavery regime, and with a little less heat and scarcely more rationality by historians since that time. Part of the confusion that has prevailed has been a confusion of issues. The relative cost or economic efficiency of slave or free labor to a master or employer is quite a different question from that of general sectional advantages under one system or the other, and still different from that of general social policy in accordance with some set of ethical values. An examination of the first of these questions involves no answer to the other two.

Much of the argument during the slavery period about slave-free labor may be dismissed as irrelevant, since it was concerned with sectional advantages. Other arguments have overlooked essential facts in the situation. For example, under the circumstances in the South, the question of Negro slave labor *versus* free White labor was largely meaningless. Free White labor was during the colonial period never a serious competitor with White servitude or Negro servitude. The abundance of land created a condition whereby it was impossible to obtain enough White laborers, at any price, for large-scale agricultural production, and the consequent wage scale of those willing to accept wage employment was too high for their profitable employment by an entrepreneur. The system of indentured servitude was the first attempted solution of this labor problem, and in the South this was supplemented and finally supplanted by Negro slavery. Slavery, then, was the established labor system of the South, just as wage labor was in the North, before voluntary prepaid immigration became of large-scale importance. For reasons to be outlined below, the slavery system was an effective barrier to a proportional immigration to the South.

The essential question is not whether the South would have been better off if its entire population had been made up of white laborers of western European origin working under the wage system; but whether the South could have employed the African Negro, after he was brought to this country, in any more effective manner; and more than this, why the Negro slave, in spite of the alleged inferiority of slavery as a method of stimulating exertion, was able to displace the economy of free small farmers.

For one thing, considering the characteristic immediacy of the primitive Negro, it is probable that the rewards and punishments of the plantation system were more powerful stimuli than the rewards and punishments of the plantation system were under a system of free labor. By no means were all slaves sullen, wretched, and driven cattle, working only under the lash. On the smaller plantations, especially, they felt an interest in the affairs of the plantation, and their advice was not infrequently asked by the master. In many cases they took pride in the master's wealth and prosperity, tacitly accepting the position of inferiority and subordination—a position that probably caused them little sorrow.

Slavery as an industrial system possessed certain positive advantages even as compared with the system of wage labor. From the standpoint of the employer, slavery provided a stable labor supply. Barring ordinary accidents and sickness, the laborer's services were always available—an important advantage in large-scale farming. There was probably a certain degree of economic inelasticity in the supply of labor, particularly at harvest-time, when there was little surplus labor except children, and slave labor flowed less readily than free labor to the type of employment promising greatest economic opportunity, due partly to the difficulties in transferring the capital values of the slave's labor. As compared with serfdom, however, slavery possessed the manifest advantage that the laborer could be moved to the point of greatest productive advantage, while the serf was bound to a particular manor. It was found practicable to employ slave women in field labor, as well as men, while throughout America custom did not ordinarily sanction the employment of white women in the fields. Furthermore, it was practicable to use child labor from a comparatively early age in such activities as worming and suckering tobacco and picking cotton. Slavery involved no problem of unemployment, and the system bred no lockouts, blacklists, and strikes.[32]

The related question of slave *versus* free, independent labor, is necessarily complicated by the fact that whatever competition actually took place was between plantations with slave labor, and small-scale diversified farms (or even those growing a single staple crop) operated by independent White yeomen. The concrete historical question at issue, therefore, was not the labor system alone, but the competitive efficiency of types and degrees of economic organization. Under the given circumstances slave labor was not economically inferior to free labor.

The economically relevant factors and relationships in the plantation-slavery regime were not, of course, static. Once the combination of a method of agricultural exploitation and a method of labor exploitation was achieved, or rather set in motion, certain aspects of subsequent economic development were already implied.[33] Thus, in the dynamics of this configuration, it is meaningful to ask: (1) What were the concrete historical tendencies of economic development? (2) To what extent did these tendencies or changes follow from the functional interrelation of factors proper to the system of economic relationships?

In a commercial economy such as the production of agricultural staples in the South, the trend of the market price in relation to labor costs is significant. Thus the relation of cotton prices to the price of slaves in Southern markets has been taken by economic historians as an index of the trend in the economic soundness of the plantation-slavery regime. An examination of the relationship may serve both to point up some of the characteristic features of the development of the economic organization and to provide a basis for examination of some interpretations hitherto given that development.

COMMODITIES DOWN; LABOR UP

Although the comparison of slave prices with only the prices of cotton neglects other important staple crops (tobacco, rice, and sugar), the production of cotton represented such a major proportion of the commercial agriculture that this error of omission should not be of decisive importance. The supremacy of the slavery-cotton combination was in this respect so marked that variations in the prices for "prime field hands" for cotton plantations necessarily affected the prices of that minority of slaves required for other plantation crops. Since cotton plantations represented the principal market for slaves, other buyers had at least to meet the price cotton planters were willing to pay, in local markets. Moreover, temporarily greater prosperity in the minor staples could only affect prices for slaves slightly and locally, because, unlike cotton, the conditions for great expansion were absent. Thus in a "real" as well as in a symbolic manner, the "Kingdom of Cotton" dominated lesser principalities.

The most complete study of slave and cotton prices, from primary materials, has been made by Phillips. For cotton prices he has used monthly or annual averages of market quotations in the principal cotton trading centers. Phillips relies primarily on New York prices. (A chart of New York and Liverpool prices in Hammond,[34] shows a very close conformity between the two markets from 1820 to 1860. From 1800 to 1820 there is a conformity in fluctuations and trend, but a fairly wide disparity in price, Liverpool quotations being considerably higher. Average slave prices, or prices of "prime field hands" are more difficult to determine because of the inadequacy of contemporary sources, and lack of a definite market organization. However, large quantities of bills of sale recording actual market transactions afford, Phillips thinks, reasonably accurate averages.[35]

Although these data and estimates show some short-term uniformity of fluctuations in slave and cotton prices, there was a marked long-term downward trend in cotton prices and a long-term upward trend in slave prices. This requires explanation. Phillips' own explanation is in terms of a sort of irrational speculation, with an ". . . irresistible tendency to overvalue and overcapitalize slave labor . . ."[36] But we should not overlook economic and technical interpretations.

Cotton prices declined through greater efficiency and smaller cost of production. Improvements were constantly being made in cultivating, ginning and marketing the staple. The increase in slave prices reflected the increasing efficiency and productivity of slave labor due to the fact that after the official elimination of slave importation in 1808 an ever-increasing proportion of the slave population was native-born and trained from infancy in the slavery regime. (Illegal imports of slaves continued, estimated to have been from four to eight thousand a year. The subterfuges or bribes necessary to keep up the unlawful commerce would of course add to costs.[37])

There was also a steady improvement and greater efficiency in management due to the definite trend toward the ideal-typical plantation system.

More important than either the improved qualities of slaves or increased commercialization was the fact that in an expanding commercial economy the demand for labor outran the supply. Further slave importations were limited by the legal prohibition, and the natural increase of the slave population was insufficient to supply the demand. The slavery regime proved to be an effective barrier to supplying the deficiency through voluntary White immigration.

It is in reference to the two objective market conditions of cotton and slave prices that the characteristic features of the dynamics of the plantation-slavery system are to be understood. Thus the significance of "soil exhaustion," and its concomitant, the "necessity of expansion," depends upon these changing market conditions. As previously indicated, soil exhaustion under the plantation-slavery system was not absolute. As Gray writes, "Broadly speaking, Southern soils were 'exhausted' in the sense that annual yields had been reduced to the point where it was more profitable to abandon old land and apply labor and capital to fresh lands." [38] Although the fertility of plantation soils was depleted in the absolute sense, through improper cultivation, soil erosion, and the "one-crop system" of agriculture, it may with some justice be said that all of these factors were simply functions of the abundance of land. With fresh lands being opened on the Southern or Western frontier, it was cheaper to move than to improve. The cheapness and abundance of land removed a large part of operating expenses represented by upkeep. Planters were relieved of the necessity of growing non-commercial crops for soil restoration, and of diverting their labor force to the non-productive work (in the immediate sense) of manuring and other methods of maintaining soil resources.[39] The lands became "exhausted" then only in the sense that a greater return on capital (land and labor) could be earned elsewhere.

The availability, and occupation, of land to the south and west, however, had an even more decisive effect upon "soil exhaustion" and upon the alleged necessity for expansion as reflected in the declining prices of cotton, and advancing prices of slaves. The greater productivity of the plantations of the Southwest, due not only to greater soil fertility, but also to a greater efficiency and closer approach to the ideal-typical plantation-slavery combination, meant that the planters could produce more cotton at a lower price, and at the same time compete successfully for the services of a limited labor supply. This interregional competition had the effect of reducing or eliminating the profits of the plantation-slavery regime in the older regions. Gray, as usual, is bitingly incisive on these points:

The large differential in productivity stimulated the transfer of slave labor to the Southwest, either by sale or by migration. The compulsion came about through the fact that the newer regions were able to capitalize slave labor so high that in the regions of early settlement it could not earn interest at the market rate at these higher capital values. It was in this sense that the employment of slave labor in general farming was frequently unprofitable. In the same sense, it was unprofitable when employed in the production of cotton in some of the older cotton producing regions. It could not produce a surplus sufficiently large to pay interest on the high capital values made possible by competition of regions where slave labor was employed to better advantage. Nevertheless, slave labor of the older regions—probably even in colonial New England—was able to earn a surplus above the cost of maintenance, and had it not been for the competition of the new lands of the west, it would have continued profitable in the older regions as long as it was possible to average something above cost of subsistence.

It was the fact that slavery tended to be profitable in new regions, while unprofitable in regions in the wake of expansion, that resulted so generally in the mistaken conclusion, that slavery can thrive only on the basis of geographical expansion and a migratory economy, that slavery is adapted only to extensive agriculture, that it inevitably results in soil exhaustion, and that it cannot be profitable in general farming; none of which conclusions . . . appears to be justified in the absolute sense in which it has been asserted.

It will be apparent also that the idea that the interest on the capital value of slaves was a necessary element in cost of production is true only in the sense that, being earned by one region or industry, it must be paid by other regions and industries in order to command the services of labor. In a general sense, however, this surplus was not a necessary charge. If the prices of all the Southern products had fallen so low that it was impossible in any industry or region to earn more than a few dollars a year as the net return for slave labor, it would still have been advantageous to employ it.[40]

EXPANSION: INSTITUTIONALIZED IRRATIONALITY

These considerations throw a new light upon the presumed necessity of expansion, as an inherent characteristic of the plantation-slavery system. During the slavery period the plantation system had utilized only a fraction of the available land area. Expansion into the most fertile and most favorably located lands was a continued necessity, not because of the characteristic weaknesses of the plantation system with slave labor, but because, in the first instance, of an inadequate supply of slave labor. The continually rising slave prices brought about by a demand exceeding the supply caused slavery to be unprofitable on the older, less fertile lands. In this sense the older soils became "exhausted" so far as the profitable growing of the staple crop with expensive labor was concerned. (The process may well have hastened soil exhaustion in the absolute sense as well. It seems reasonable to suppose that interregional competition would force a more thoroughly exploitive economy in the less-favored region before production was abandoned.) But this effective demand for slave labor itself came as a result of geographical expansion to the south and west. In short, the whole process became a sort of circle. Paradoxical as it may seem, the characteristic "soil exhaustion," mobility, and the necessity for continued expansion *came about largely as a result of the possibility of expansion.* This conclusion is further corroborated by the fact that the plantation-slavery system, in areas where expansion was impossible, did not "exhaust" the soils or become "strangled for lack of room to expand." Although subject to the market price for slaves, largely determined by the demand of cotton planters, the rice, sea-island cotton, and sugar plantations were not subject to interregional competition in marketing their staple. Since they could not expand, and did not "need" to expand because of falling returns from their labor force, they attempted to maintain soil resources. An even better comparative case, because not subject to American slave prices, is provided by the plantations of the British West Indies, where, with land at a premium, soils were kept up and improved. Yet the slavery system was abolished by law, not by economic necessity.[41]

Under this necessity of expansion, which was real enough, although not inherent in the plantation-slavery economy, two notable changes took place in Southern economic life. The geographical sphere of slavery was broadened and extended to the south and southwest. At the same time changes were being produced in the plantation-slavery economy, both in the vanguard and in the wake of expansion.

[It will be recalled that in 1790 around four-fifths of the slaves in the South were in the border states, over three-fifths in Virginia and Maryland alone. The introduction of cotton, and the beginning of the "expansionist" movement resulted in the first instance in extending the area of plantation agriculture into the Piedmont region. From the Virginia Piedmont the movement was southward to the Carolinas and Georgia, the "Old Cotton Belt," and subsequently along the Gulf coast, into and across the Mississippi lowlands, the "New Cotton Belt."] Both the direction and volume of this movement may perhaps best be seen in a tabulation of the percentage of increase of the slave populations in the various Southern states during the period. Table I shows these percentages. [It will be noted that by 1800 the movement out of Delaware, Maryland, and Virginia was well under way, both to the transmontane border states of Kentucky and Tennessee, and to the Deep South. Between 1800 and 1810 the plantation-slavery regime had spread along the Gulf coast to the Mississippi, and subsequently to Louisiana, Arkansas, and Missouri, then into Florida after its acquisition by the United States, and finally into Texas, after its annexation.]It will also be observed that the opening of a new territory typically produced a large percentage increase in the slave population between the first two census enumerations, and a subsequent "coasting off" in succeeding enumerations. This is, of course, partially misleading since a relatively small numerical increase in the slave population will show a very large percentage increase at the second enumeration, if the slave population was extremely small at the first enumeration. However, due to the great mobility of Southern agricultural production, and the natural tendency of those planters who arrived first to take the most favorable lands and locations, the most rapid expansion in a new territory

TABLE I

PER CENT INCREASE OF THE SLAVE POPULATION OF THE SLAVE STATES AT EACH CENSUS: 1790 TO 1860*

State	1790 to 1800	1800 to 1810	1810 to 1820	1820 to 1830	1830 to 1840	1840 to 1850	1850 to 1860
Delaware	−30.8	−32.1	7.9	−27.0	−20.9	−12.1	−21.5
Maryland	4.5	6.8	−2.7	−3.0	−13.4	1.1	−3.9
Virginia	18.6	13.7	8.3	10.4	−4.5	4.9	3.9
North Carolina	32.3	26.7	21.4	19.9	0.1	17.4	14.7
South Carolina	36.5	34.4	31.6	32.0	3.7	17.7	4.5
Georgia	103.0	77.1	42.2	45.4	29.2	35.9	21.1
Florida	—	—	—	—	65.9	52.0	57.1
Kentucky	224.0	99.7	57.3	30.4	10.3	15.8	6.9
Tennessee	297.5	227.8	79.9	76.8	29.3	30.8	15.1
Alabama	—	419.2	1532.7	180.7	115.7	35.2	26.9
Mississippi	—	384.9	125.9	100.1	197.3	58.7	40.9
Louisiana	—	—	99.3	58.7	65.7	45.3	35.5
Arkansas	—	—	1089.0	185.0	335.6	136.3	135.9
Texas	—	—	—	—	—	—	213.9
Missouri	—	—	256.6	145.5	132.1	50.1	31.5

* Adapted from U.S. Bureau of the Census, *A Century of Population Growth* (Washington: Government Printing Office, 1904), p. 134, Table 61.

undoubtedly did take place within the first ten or fifteen years of its availability.

THE PRODUCTION OF SLAVES FOR THE MARKET

What was happening in the geographical redistribution of slaves was relatively simple if not exactly pretty. It became more profitable, in the old slave states, to raise slaves rather than to depend primarily on cash crops such as tobacco or rice or even to raise cotton on "exhausted" lands in competition with new lands. Naturally, a considerable attempt was made to keep slaves profitably employed until sold. There were probably few genuine "stud farms," yet the early movement out of Virginia, Delaware and Maryland to the Carolinas, Kentucky, and Tennessee was followed by a period when the net importers became net exporters to the Southwest. Among the older states and regions, Georgia alone escaped loss of slaves through competition of the newer regions. This was no doubt partially due to the continued importance of the minor staples of rice and sea-island cotton, and to the fact that throughout the period its plantation economy continued on a large scale.

The increased importance of the slavery regime in the newer areas may also be seen by comparing the percentage increase and the proportion of the total slaves in the original area (1790) and added areas. By 1860, fully half of the total slave population in the South was in the area added to the United States after the first census.[42]

Another index of the area of expansion and increased importance of slavery is the relative market prices of slaves in various regional markets. The data assembled by Phillips[43] on four Southern markets (Virginia, Charleston, Georgia, and New Orleans) indicate that from 1800 to 1860 slave prices were uniformly highest in New Orleans, lowest in Virginia, Charleston and Georgia being intermediate, with an increasing disparity for the high-priced markets. In fact, the lowest price at any given time was that at the most northern of the four markets, with prices progressively higher to the south and west. This price differential (representing essentially differential place utility) serves to confirm the direction of slave movements.

THE ECONOMIES OF SCALE

The geographical movement of the plantation-slavery system has implied a simple transfer of plantations of an average size to new territories, or the selling of slaves to new territories. The typical pattern of movement was more complex, however. It was not the large plantation owner who moved first, but the small planter or farmer. The large plantation owner was better able to manage his cropping and withstand minor disasters or price declines. The farmer was continually moving to the edge of the frontier, with increasing self-sufficiency, but followed by the planters, with the whole development repeated. The end product, in the wake of expansion, was sometimes industrial diversification, sometimes partial depopulation of some districts.[44] The economy of the South was commercial, and therefore highly competitive. The competition, moreover, was not inter-regional alone, for it was severe between planters and farmers, and between large plantation owners and small plantation owners. In this competition the large plantation owner had certain real advantages. The labor force could be managed with the minimum expense and maximum efficiency. With a large labor force, the risk of loss through the death of slaves was decreased. Some plantation machinery was almost a "fixed cost," and therefore operated to the advantage of the planter who had the largest output. The large plantation owner could more easily secure credit, and his purchases in large quantities secured him the most favorable terms. In short, with variation in details, he had the advantages of any large enterpriser over a smaller one. These advantages, combined with a more careful cultivation of the soil, made it possible for the large planter to withstand "soil exhaustion" longer than the small planter or the independent farmer. He could buy out his neighbors and increase his land and labor force. If he finally moved, he was still in a position to buy out those who preceded him.[45]

The spatial dynamics of the plantation-slavery system was thus accompanied by organizational changes: the growth and increasing importance of the larger ideal-typical plantation-slavery organization. This meant in concrete terms a relative decrease in the number of slaveholders, and, a corollary, an increase in the number of slaves per slaveholder—the concentration of wealth. The general pattern of this movement throughout the period has been summarized by Phillips:

> The average size of slaveholdings tended to increase with moderation in ordinary periods, while in periods of either marked prosperity or severe depression there was nearly always a stimulated growth of the larger slaveholdings and a thinning out of the small ones, and hence a quickened growth in the size of the average slaveholding.
>
> The *aggregate* number of slaveholdings tended to increase or decrease according to the stage of development which the community had reached. That is, so long as population was scanty and opportunity abundant, the small producers as well as the large ones flowed in. But when the land had become more completely occupied and opportunity restricted, an outflow would begin, and the smallest units would lead the exodus. Both flush times and hard times quickened this fluctuation of the total of units, merely hastening movements which were already in progress.[46]

Organizational change accompanied the geographic shift of slavery, so that as slavery moved into the Deep South and Southwest it became increasingly a large-scale commercial arrangement. In the older border states, on the other hand, the exodus of the labor force and the failure in competition with the newer regions engendered a shift from a large-scale plantation economy to diversified farming. Thus in the regions where slavery and the plantation system were most vigorous, the large planter supplanted the smaller planter and increased his labor force. The regions in the wake of this expansion largely abandoned the typical plantation-slavery system in favor of a less completely commercial economy. For the slave-holding states of the South, the proportion of slaves to total population remained about constant at one-third during the entire 1790–1860 period, with the combined slave-holding population declining from almost three-fifths to one-half. In the Border States the proportion of slavery declined from two-fifths to just over one-fifth. In the Lower South, the proportions of slaves increased from around 41 per cent to around 45. The total population was of course also shifting, but by 1860 a remarkable 64.5 per cent of that Lower South population was directly involved in the slavery system. Darkies may have been strumming banjos under the magnolia trees in Virginia, but field hands were being commercially exploited in Mississippi, Louisiana, Texas, and Arkansas.[47] Pg. 180 lxxviii

The historical dynamics of the commercial economy of the South during the slavery period shows, then, not only the interregional competitive advantages of the areas of greatest commercial development (the areas of expansion) but also the local competitive efficiency of the large plantation owner. As far as the profitability of slavery to the individual slaveholder is concerned, the situation is clear-cut. In the competitive order, the planter who operated a large plantation with slave labor could outbid the independent farmer for land, and outbid the smaller planter for land and labor. Moreover, he could undersell both in the staple markets. Slavery was in 1860 by no means an economically decadent institution.

Private Gain and Public Loss

The question of the individual profitability of slavery is, however, quite distinct from its economic advantage to the South as a whole. Although soil exploitation and exhaustion were not products of slavery, but of an abundance of natural resources, certain other disadvantages did accrue to the South as a result of slavery. Slavery was a very effective barrier to free White immigration, and therefore caused a shortage of labor, especially in the regions in the wake of expansion. Labor was too dear for experimentation in industrial diversification. Specialization resulted in an inadequate or wasteful utilization of natural resources. But perhaps more important than any of these was the fact that slavery resulted in an inadequate utilization of the labor resources already on hand. Phillips held this opinion:

The prevalence of the plantation regime stratified industrial society, and society in general, to a greater degree than was expedient for developing the greatest resources and power from the population on hand. In particular, while it utilized the productive strength of the Negro population to excellent effect, it substantially discouraged the non-planter whites and thereby reduced their service to the world and to themselves.[48]

There is, of course, no basis for concluding that the slavery system utilized the full productive capacities of the Negro slaves. That is only Phillips' racism showing again. The limits to the development of economic abilities and skills among slaves were definite, and had no necessary reference to their inherent capabilities. It was as unthinkable for a Negro slave to do "white men's work" as it was for a non-slaveholding White to do "nigger's work." This meant on the one hand that many "poor whites" were shut off from *any* honorable employment (and therefore, usually, of any employment at all except bare independent self-sufficiency), and, on the other hand, that many Negro slaves were prevented from escaping their "dishonorable" employment. Both situations were due to the slavery and caste system, and both militated against full utilization of the productive capacities of the labor supply. For although slavery may in a certain sense be said to have been basically an economic system of labor organization, it was not exclusively so. It could only operate within a legal and institutional framework that defined the status of slaves and freemen as persons, in addition to their roles as laborers in an economic organization. And it was essentially this legal and institutional definition of status that had wider ramifications for the region as a whole. Some of these ramifications affected the regional economy of the South, and it is only in reference to the non-economic factors in the relationships of production that the paradox of a system individually profitable and unprofitable in net result disappears.

IV

The Legal Status
of Slavery*

Negroes were first introduced into the American colonies as an addition to the labor force provided by the White indentured servants already imported. The conditions of servitude of Negroes so imported were at first regulated by local law as in the case of involuntary White servants. That is, local legislation prescribed the term of service of convicts, kidnapped persons, and Negroes, none of whom had indenture contracts. Negroes, after all, were exported from Africa as slaves, not as voluntary emigrants with or without contracts. This "original" status subsequently became important in the legalization and ideological defense of slavery, as we shall later note. But in the continental British colonies, those Negroes that arrived early were subject to indenture laws, there being neither contracts on the one hand, or slave laws on the other. The inden-

* A variant of this chapter was published as "Slave Law and Social Structure," *Journal of Negro History,* 26:171–202, April 1941.

ture laws served to maintain the *fiction* of a legal contractual obligation, and this fiction applied to unwilling black servants as well as it did to Whites. But in the case of both Whites and blacks, the absence of an oral or written contract made the fiction at times difficult to maintain, and it was not unknown for White servants in this situation to be forced into a "life indenture." [1] Since all Negroes were imported without indenture, a similar policy in regard to Negro servants appears to have been the beginning of a gradual differentiation in the status of White and Negro servants. Slavery was not originally established by law in any American colony, but its development by custom was later recognized by legislation. It was this recognition and the subsequent increase in the precision of definition of the legal status of slavery that gave this type of labor relationship its effective advantages over indentured servitude.

Although the confirmation of slavery as the legal status of the Negro servant was crucial for subsequent commercial and industrial development in the South, there is little evidence that some type of Negro slavery should have been a crucial issue at the time, in view of the fact that "Moors" and Negroes had been subject to the slave trade long before the settlement of the American colonies. (Aside from the strictly intra-African and especially Islamic slave trade, Pope Nicholas V in 1452 empowered the king of Portugal to sell into slavery "all Moslems, heathen and other foes of Christ," and that merely confirmed a practice of several years' standing.) Yet it is clear that in the case of any innovation, legal decision and policy will be based in the first instance upon existent local law. Thus the failure immediately to fix legal slavery as proper for imported Negroes was partially due to the previous establishment of the system of indentured servitude. The gradual, customary enslavement of Negro servants was in the first instance simply a reversion to a policy previously established elsewhere, and was undoubtedly facilitated by that fact. This inference is borne out by the conformity of the early colonial expositions of the legal bases for slavery with the previously established rules and practices of the slave-trading powers.

EARLY JUSTIFICATIONS OF SLAVERY

The current legal justifications of slavery were of three sorts, so closely related that they were often not distinguished: just wars, status quo ante, and heathenism. The first of these justifications, usually in connection with the third, had long been claimed as grounds for enslavement.[2] Although this principle was used by the colonists in justification of the enslavement of Indians, it could be applied only indirectly in the case of Negroes, since the colonists themselves had no opportunity of waging "just wars" against them. (The enslavement of Indians was apparently practiced in all colonies to a limited extent, but abandoned for a variety of reasons, chiefly: the difficulty of reducing Indians to forced servile labor; the ease with which they escaped to their fellows: the injury thereby done to hopes of peaceful relations with the natives.[3])

When the "just wars" argument was used, therefore, it was in justification of the *original* enslavement of the Negroes. Much more pertinent to the colonists was the argument that the Negroes imported as slaves were *already* slaves either before coming into the hands of the traders, or at least before offered for sale in the colonies.

Much of the early legal justification of Negro slavery involved "passing the buck." The planter bought from a local trader or factor, who bought from a Transatlantic trader, who in turn dealt either with a White factor on the African coast or directly with a native chief. None of the Whites accepted responsibility for the act of enslavement. This was held (and usually correctly) to have been accomplished already by the Africans. Pushed one step further, the original enslavement was held to have been the result of a sentence for a criminal act, or "just wars" between African natives.

The purchase of the slaves by American planters was thus regarded as a strictly commercial transaction, implying nothing as to the grounds for the original enslavement of the Negroes.[4] But this conception did not provide an adequate basis for the full development of a slavery system in colonial law, since it established neither the legal definition of the rights and obligations involved in the master-slave relationship nor in the last analysis, the determination of who might be slaves. The common law provided no answer to either question, and solution therefore depended on local adjudication or legislation, based either on the (legally recognized) practice of European slave-trading nations, or upon local innovations. The argument that Negroes imported as slaves were already slaves before being imported did not alter the fact that the law recognized no such relationship, nor the fact that slavery was thus limited to Negroes, and under no circumstances extended to Europeans. Although there is no record of colonial cases arising which were determined in reference to the third current justification of enslavement of Negroes, there is ample evidence that the "heathen" condition of Negroes was in fact relied upon as justification of the practice. This legal justification had been held in Europe to apply to enslaving Mohammedan Moors and also Negroes.[5]

THE PROBLEM OF CONVERSION

Now the justification of slavery on the basis of the heathen condition of the enslaved raises an obvious problem of the status of the slave after conversion.[6] It is precisely in reference to this problem that the acceptance in the American colonies of the "heathenism" justification is evident, and the evidence arises, ironically enough, from legislative denial of freedom or enfranchisement through conversion. The first such act recorded was passed by Maryland in 1664, with the avowed purpose of preventing damage to masters from slaves claiming freedom on the basis of conversion.[7] Virginia followed shortly with an act (1667) stating in part, "That the conferring of baptisms doth not alter the condition of the person as to his bondage or freedom, that divers masters, freed from this doubt, may more carefully endeavor the propagation of christianity." [8] Catterall, in discussing this early problem of the status of the converted, points out that the principle of enfranchisement of baptized slaves was already established in England, and apparently early adopted in the American colonies. She moreover suggests that a possible reason for the failure immediately to establish slavery as the status of the first Negroes in the colonies was that possibly these came from Spanish dominions and were already baptized (as evidenced by the record of names, which are largely Spanish in form).[9] That the problem of conversion continued to arise, despite this early legislation, is evident from the number of times colonial legislatures repeated denials of freedom through conversion. Following the act of 1664 in Maryland, three additional enactments appear in colonial legislation; in Virginia, the denial was repeated four times after the act of 1667, the last one as late as 1748. Other colonies, beginning such legislation at a later period, apparently found repetition less necessary.[10] The explanatory preambles of all these acts, stating the purpose and necessity of the laws, were typified by the first Virginia and Maryland acts. That is, the two principal conditions which it was the purpose of the laws to prevent were that masters were refusing to let their slaves become converted, thus hindering the spread of Christianity and converted slaves were being freed, thus causing loss to their owners. Some of the laws cited the one condition, some the other. If the stated purposes of the legislation be taken at their face value, they may appear to be absolutely different, perhaps antithetical, in motivation. However, more careful analysis will reveal that actually the conditions to be eliminated were simply two sides of the same problem. That problem was that, in view of the acceptance of the ethical or moral conviction making conversion and slave status incompatible, there was a conflict between profitable slavery and the spread of Christianity. Although the removal of this restriction may be said to be evidence of the pressure of economic interests upon an ethical conception, there seems to be no reason to insist that the "real" or "true" interest involved in the legislation was economic, and the expressed interest in the conversion of the Negroes was just a "rationalization." The removal of the rule that freedom followed conversion simply made the two formerly conflicting interests of conversion and slavery compatible.

Perhaps the legislation in Virginia is most interesting, since it shows a more or less gradual shifting from the justification arising from the heathen condition of the slave to the heathen background or origin of the slaves. The act of 1670 exempted from slavery those who were already converted before importation, whereas the acts of 1682 and 1705 exempted only those who were Christians in their native country, or free in some Christian country before their importation. The practical effect of this was to forge a definitive link between Negro ancestry and legal slavery. A number of colonial acts, not dealing with the problem of conversion and baptism, illustrate the tendency to distinguish Negroes (or slaves) and Christians as general and exclusive categories, without regard to the Christian or pagan status of individual Negroes.[11] These acts prohibit such actions as a Negro threatening to strike a Christian, miscegenation between Negroes and Christians, and testifying by Negroes against Christians.

The legislation, and repeated legislation, concerning the status of converted slaves points clearly to a persistent difficulty in establishing the ethics of slavery. The conception that slavery, as a legal relation between Christian persons, was incompatible with the Christian ethic died hard. Although the particular point at issue —slavery or freedom for converted slaves—was settled in favor of continued slavery, and remained so determined throughout the slavery regime, part of the ethical conflict involved remained. In particular, the question of the essential nature of the slavery relationship was at stake, and was never definitively determined. Two alternative explanations were possible: either the master-slave relationship was simply a particular property relationship, or else it was a legal relationship between legal persons. Conversion of a slave to Christianity inevitably admitted him to be a person, and despite legal definitions in terms of property, the conception remained ambivalent.

From Heathenism to Racialism

The justification of Negro slavery on the basis of the original "heathenish" state of Negroes in Africa, and without regard to subsequent conversion of individual slaves to Christianity, also provided the basis for a distinctively American legal justification —the inherent racial inferiority of the Negroes. Although it is true, as Hurd points out, that the confinement of the slave trade by European nations to "heathen" nations did in fact limit that trade to Indians, African Moors, and Negroes, there is no evidence to support his contention that this meant a recognition by the European countries of a racial basis for slavery.[12] In fact, the evidence from the methods of carrying on the trade indicates the exact contrary. Among the English, French, Dutch, and Portuguese traders in Africa, the political equality and local sovereignty of the natives was not questioned. Trading posts, forts, and "factories" were erected on leased land, and customs, fees, and duties were payable to the local chiefs. Slave trading was carried on through these local chiefs, and the trade was simply regarded as a profitable commerce in those already enslaved by local law and custom, and involving no position as to the inherent inferiority of the slave.[13]

The idea of racial inferiority certainly did not appear in colonial law with the introduction of Negroes. Slavery was not their status at first, either in law or in custom. It must also be clear from the preceding discussion that the legal determination and justification of who might be slaves developed slowly. Now it seems reasonable to suppose that the legal conceptions, which had the practical effect of limiting slavery to Negroes, together with the process of pushing back the religious justification to the original heathenish condition of the Negro people, upon which the conversion of the individual slave had no bearing, were directly related to the idea that slavery rested upon an inherent inferiority of the enslaved. For if slavery was in fact confined to those who quite obviously were different in appearance, and justified on the basis of the slaves' inferior background as a people, not as individuals, it is a very short step to the position that slavery is justified as a status properly attaching to a different and inferior people.

That is precisely what happened.

Without specific legislative declarations of the doctrine of racial inferiority, its rise and development may yet be traced through two types of legislation which clearly imply and rest upon the idea of racial inferiority: laws preventing inter-racial miscegenation, and laws establishing civil and legal disabilities applying to free Negroes, or to all Negroes, regardless of status. The texts of these laws and other legislative acts should provide a basis for examination of the development of a doctrine of racial inferiority, and also a test of the thesis that this doctrine of inherent inferiority is related to the "last stand" of the religious justification of slavery.

A summary of colonial legislation affecting sexual unions between Whites and Negroes, arranged chronologically, and with interpretation, may serve to outline the development of an inferiority doctrine.[14] (The summary relates only to colonial legislation, as by common-law procedure the state courts followed prior laws and decisions, following the doctrine of *stare decisis*— let the decision stand. We shall see that legislation superseded true common law, that is judicial decisions, as slavery had no basis in that law.)

1630. *Virginia.* Resolution meting out punishment to one Hugh Davis, "for abusing himself to the dishonor of God and the shame of Christians by defiling his body in lying with a negro." (229) Clearly a Christian-heathen union was here in question.

1640. *Virginia.* "Robert Sweet, to do penance in church, according to the laws of England, for getting a negro woman with child . . ." (229) Again apparently a religious question.

1663. *Maryland.* Condemns free-born women to slavery if they marry Negro slaves, "forasmuch as divers free-born *English* women, forgetful of their free condition, and to the disgrace of our nation, do intermarry with negro slaves, by which also divers suits may arise, touching the issue of such women, and a great damage doth befall the master of such Negroes . . ." (249) This act introduces the idea of an inconsistency in marriage between slaves and free-born, and between *Negro* slaves, and *English* free-born. Although not yet necessarily implying a racial disqualification, the germ of the idea is present.

1681. *Maryland.* This act, modifying the preceding one, adds to the free-born English distinction the qualification that such marriages are a disgrace not only to the English, but to "many other Christian nations," and also adds "white women." It also condemns marriages with "negroes and slaves." (280) This appears to be the first clear-cut prohibition implying racial disqualification.

1691. *Virginia.* An act "for prevention of that abominable mixture and spurious issue, which hereafter may increase in this dominion, as well by negroes, mulattoes, and Indians intermarrying with English or other white women, as by their unlawful accompanying with one another." Provides penalties for "whatsoever English or other white man or woman being free shall intermarry with a negroe, mulatto, or Indian man or woman, bond or free . . ." (236–237) This was a pattern for subsequent "racial purity" legislation.

1705. *Virginia.* Re-enacts prohibition of 1691 with a change in penalties. (240)

1705. *Massachusetts.* *"Acts for the better preventing of a spurious and mixt issue."* Prohibits marriage or sexual union between any Negro or Mulatto and an "English man, or man of any other Christian nation." (263) This would seem to be a sort of borderline between the religious and racial justification.

1716. *Maryland.* Prohibits sexual unions between Whites and Negroes. (253) In this and subsequent legislation the distinction is definitely stated to rely on the color line.

1717. *Maryland.* Prohibition similar to preceding act, but provides for life slavery for Negroes or Mulattoes who break the law. (253)

1717. *South Carolina.* Provides limited servitude for Whites having or begetting children by Blacks. (301–302)

1721. *Delaware.* Provides penalties for White women bearing Mulatto children, or White men having sexual union with Negro or Mulatto women. (292)

1725. *Pennsylvania.* Prohibition of and penalties for marriage or sexual union between Whites and Blacks. (290)

1741. *South Carolina.* Provides penalties for "White persons intermarrying with any Negro, musbee, or mulatto man or woman, or any person of mixt blood to the third generation bond or free . . ." (295)

Legislation placing disabilities upon free Negroes, despite their free condition, was of two principal types: that which intended to prevent their becoming too numerous, indigent, or providing a source of trouble to the maintenance of slavery, through instigating and aiding revolt, or simply by their presence; that which legislated against them as Negroes, members of an inferior caste, not entitled to all privileges and immunities of *white* freemen. It is the latter general type of colonial legislation which is of present interest in showing the development of the doctrine of racial inferiority. This legislation, with my commentary, is summarized below.[15]

1670. *Virginia.* Enacted that "no negro or Indian, though baptized and enjoying their own freedom," shall be capable of purchasing any Christian servants, "but yet not debarred from buying any of their own nation." (233) The prohibition against purchase of a Christian servant apparently refers to a *White* Christian servant, but the line of demarcation is still put in religious terms.

1705. *Virginia.* Negro, Mulatto, or Indian may not hold office, but may still vote (if free). (233) Another act in this year reaffirms the prohibition enacted in 1670, adding Jews, Moors, Mohametans to those not allowed to purchase "any Christian servant nor any other except of their own complexion . . ." (239–240) These acts make the implication of inferiority more obvious, and introduce the color line.

1706. *Massachusetts.* Provides penalty of severe whipping for "any negro or mulatto presuming to smite or strike an English person, or of other Christian nation . . ." (263) Although the distinction is stated in terms of membership in a Christian nation by the Whites, the germs of racial distinction are evident from the provision against *any* Negro or Mulatto, *presuming* to strike one of the dominant caste.

1713. *New Jersey.* Limits manumission because free Negroes were found to be "an idle and slothful people . . ." Provides that no Negro, Mulatto, or Indian that shall thereafter be made free shall hold any real estate in his own right. (284) This is a reservation of a symbolically important privilege to the dominant caste.

1716. *South Carolina.* Extends the vote to every White man "and no other," being a Christian, of the proper age, and having certain property. (301) This act draws the color line clearly in regard to political privileges.

1717. *Maryland.* Disbars all Negroes and Mulattoes, whether slave or free, from giving "good and valid evidence in law, in any matter or thing whatsoever . . . wherein any Christian white person is concerned." Admits their evidence against one another, except in cases "extending to depriving of life or member." (252–253)

1723. *Virginia.* Deprives every free Negro, Mulatto, or Indian, of the right to vote at any election. (242)

1725. *Pennsylvania.* Finds free Negroes "idle, slothful people," restricts manumission, and provides servitude for those who neglect to work, and loiter and misspend their time. (289–290)

1732. *Virginia.* "And whereas Negroes, mulattoes, and Indians, have lately been frequently allowed to give testimony as lawful witnesses in the general court and other courts of this colony when they have professed themselves to be Christians, and been able to give some account of the principles of the Christian religion; but forasmuch as they are people of such base and corrupt natures that the credit of their testimony cannot certainly be depended upon, and some juries have altogether rejected their evidence and others have given full credit thereto . . . ," any Negro, Mulatto, or Indian, whether slave or free, is disabled to be a witness except on the trial of a slave for a capital offense. (242)

1740. *South Carolina.* Extends the special court, without jury, provided for trials of slaves to free Negroes, and declares certain acts when committed by slaves or free Negroes to be felonies. (306)

1767. *Delaware.* Finds that free Negroes are "idle and slothful" and limits manumission. (293)

The two preceding summaries of legislation implying racial inferiority of the Negro and justification of slavery on that basis conform fairly closely chronologically, and appear to bear out the thesis that this doctrine was arising during the latter part of the seventeenth and early eighteenth centuries, at about the same time that the religious justification was held to apply to Negroes as a people, not as individuals.

The development of this doctrine of racial inequality must certainly have been enhanced by the evident physiological contrasts, especially the visibility provided by skin color. Moreover, it is probable that a great many of those Negroes freshly imported from Africa were in fact of "barbarous, wild, savage natures" [16] by colonial standards. (Probably not by much, however; the colonists were, by other reports, civilized only by rather loose but pretentious standards.)

The disfranchisement of free Negroes by the Virginia law of 1723 was questioned by the Lords Commissioners of Trade whose counsel, Richard West, could not "see why one freeman should be used worse than another, merely upon account of his complexion." [17] In 1735 Lieutenant-Governor Gooch replied with an uncompromising defense of the law. After recounting that the law was passed following the discovery of a slave conspiracy in which free Negroes and mulattoes were suspected of having a part, although there is no legal proof, he goes on

. . . yet such was the insolence of the free negroes at that time, that the next Assembly thought it necessary, not only to make the meetings of the slaves very penal, but to fix a perpetual brand upon free Negroes and mulattoes by excluding them from that great privilege of a Freeman, well knowing they always did, and ever will adhere to and favour the slaves. And 'tis likewise said to have been done with design, which I must think a good one, to make the free Negros sensible that a distinction ought to be made between their offspring and the descendants of an Englishman, with whom they never were to be accounted equal. This, I confess, may seem to carry an air of severity to such as are unacquainted with the nature of negros, and the pride of a manumitted slave, who looks on himself imediately on his acquiring his freedom to be as good a man as the best of his neighbors, but especially if he is descended of a white father or mother, let them be of what mean condition soever; and as most of them are the bastards of some of the worst of our imported servants, and the convicts, it seems no ways impolitick, as well for discouraging that kind of copulation, as to preserve a decent distinction between them and their betters, to leave this mark upon them until time and education has changed the indication of their spurious extraction, and made some alteration in their morals.[18]

Thus after this period (early Eighteenth Century) the uniquely American justification of slavery in terms of the inherent inferiority of the slaves, symbolized by difference in skin color, and applying to Negroes as such, regardless of religious or civil status, was established as an accepted legal principle. This doctrine established a caste system, based on color, with slave or free status of Negroes being only incidental. The consequences of that doctrine, over two hundred years later, still haunt American society, which remains unmistakably racist in many discouraging respects.

Perhaps the most conclusive and authoritative statement of this principle in the later slavery period was that embodied in the decision of Chief Justice Taney of the United States Supreme Court in the case of Dred Scott:

They [Negroes] had for more than a century before, [the time of the Declaration of Independence and of the adoption of the Constitution of the U.S.] been regarded as beings of an inferior order, and altogether unfit to associate with the white race, either in social or political relations; and so far inferior, that they had no rights which the white man was bound to respect; and that the Negro might justly and lawfully be reduced to slavery for his benefit. He was bought and sold, and treated as an ordinary article of merchandise and traffic, whenever a profit could be made by it. This opinion was at that time fixed and universal in the civilized portion of the white race. It was regarded as an axiom in morals as well as in politics . . .[19]

This infamous decision, which many historians credit with contributing to the (probably inevitable) Civil War, by Mr. Justice Taney marks the judge as ignorant of history, racist in philosophy, and certainly a miserably bad lawyer, since all the common-law precedents were against his decision.

Later legislation and court decisions did not, of course, often hinge upon this justification of pure racism, since it was regarded as fixed. Thus, suits for freedom did not call into question the justice of Negro slavery in general, but only the legal right of the master to hold a particular slave who claimed freedom on the grounds of his own previous manumission, or the freedom of a maternal ancestor. Two types of legal fictions are recorded in court decisions, however, which may be noted for their interest in the justification of slavery. The one, which conforms to a persistent historical illusion, is that slavery was introduced and established in the colonies by the regulation of the mother country which the courts were bound to respect.[20] This doctrine is by no means borne out historically. A similar fictional justification is that from the first introduction of Negroes into the American colonies they were always held as property or at least as slaves.[21] This elementary falsehood, showing incompetence in historical scholarship, has of course been repeated by countless American historians. This doctrine appears to be comparable to the common law principle of recognition by courts of customs existing "since time immemorial, when the mind of man runneth not to the contrary." Although the legal doctrine is not supported historically, it is an important fiction not only in the legal justification of slavery, but in fixing the principle that slavery was the presumptive status of Negroes.

INHERITANCE OF SLAVERY

The establishment of the legal principle that slavery was a status properly belonging to the Negro, as inherently inferior, went far toward the legal determination of who might be slaves. But because slavery was *not* uniformly the status of Negroes from their first introduction, because not all Negroes were slaves, even after slavery was established, and finally, because anti-miscegenation laws were not in force from the first and not uniformly obeyed thereafter (with the effect that physiological criteria were variable and fallible)—for all these reasons the legal criteria of the status of slavery required further elaboration. The rule which really established the hereditary status of slavery, and provided a basis for decision in doubtful cases such as mixed parentage, was the famous principle of *partus sequitur ventrem*—the child to follow the condition of the mother.

In view of the comparatively slow development of other principles involved in the legal status of slavery, it is surprising that the principle of *partus sequitur ventrem* was enunciated so early. The first recorded law establishing the principle was that of Virginia in 1662, fixing the slave status of children born to a slave mother by an English father.[22] The inheritable quality of slavery therefore was fixed before the complete development of the legal justification for slavery. Hurd suggests this as evidence that the early conception of the slavery relationship was that of property, and not of legal persons.[23] The common law, which recognized no chattel slavery, provided the principle of following the status of the parents, or in cases of parents of different status *partus sequitur patrem*—follow the status of the father. The principle of *partus sequitur ventrem* was a rule of Roman civil law, which recognized chattel slavery.[24]

Although it is probable that other colonies followed *in practice* this early Virginia rule,[25] it is perhaps significant that other colonial *laws* enunciating the hereditary principle of slavery through the mother's status date from the time that slavery had been given, at least by implication, a racial justification.[26]

The relationship between the doctrine of racial inferiority of Negroes and the doctrine that the status of slavery was hereditary through the mother is obvious, for if slavery is a condition attaching to the Negro because of inherent (racial) inferiority, it is inheritable, even in case one parent is White. Just why there should be a distinction, in case of a mixed union, between mulattos born of a White mother and those born of a Negro mother does not, of course, become immediately evident on that basis. The explanation seems to lie in two circumstances. Apart from the "racial inferiority" doctrine, the civil law rule applying to chattel slaves determined the status of the "increase" of the females. A master who owned a female slave owned also her increase. A Mulatto born of a White woman could not come under this rule at all. The typical "race crossing" was and has remained the White male with the Negro female. Available evidence would indicate that the Mulattoes resulting from the reverse relationship were of such negligible numerical importance as to require no legislation to prevent a sizeable group from escaping slavery thereby. Indeed, the possibility that a mixed-breed child might be fathered by a Negro father, slave or free, upon a free White woman was so improbable that no laws (other than general anti-miscegenation laws) or court cases considered the situation at all. But certainly fear of the sexual prowess of the male Negro was, and has remained, a powerful force in the neurotic racism of American Whites.[27]

Presumption of Slavery from Color

The rule of *partus sequitur ventrem* fixed the method of making slavery hereditary, but it could scarcely, alone, have established a hereditary caste system. For a caste system depends primarily upon visibility or absolutely certain knowledge of lineage as a basis for assignment into the dominant or subordinate caste. The next logical step beyond the principle of racial inferiority, and legalized inheritance of status, therefore, was the correlative principle that slavery was the presumptive status of every Negro or "person of color" as evident from "inspection." In other words, a person's caste was determined by his "bearing a stamp of servility," in this case his skin color, and the necessary presumption then must be that the person's legal status as the status typical of that caste needed no further proof. Every Negro, and every person who by "inspection" could be judged to be descended from one or more Negro ancestors, was therefore assumed to be a slave, unless he could produce evidence to the contrary.

Only one colonial law directly affirming slavery as the presumptive status of the Negro or "person of color" has been found, that of South Carolina in 1740.[28] Moreover, no judicial cases affirming the principle appear in the records before the early nineteenth century.[29] It may perhaps appear surprising, in view of the "logicality" of the presumption of slavery once the *racial* inferiority doctrine was established, that so little legislative action should have been taken on the subject, and that judicial cases affirming the principle occurred so late in the slavery period. The explanation seems to lie in the fact that the principle, well-established, came to legal or judicial attention only in suits for freedom. (This was, after all, basically a common-law system. Thus there could be no presumption that the legal order would be completely articulated, including the logical implications of general principles. In fact, the general principles of slavery were antithetical to common-law precedents, and the most "conservative" courts were thus often the most hostile to the principles and only reluctantly applied legislative acts.)

The freedom suits, the only type of civil action a slave could take, did not begin until the nineteenth century. It seems plausible that abolition of slavery in the North, and the pronounced increase in manumission around the turn of the century, were at least partly responsible for cases pressing the demands for freedom of Southern slaves.

The legal presumption in freedom suits was, then, in the first instance, that any Negro or "person of color" held as a slave bore the burden of proof to establish his freedom. This he might do if he could show a free maternal ancestor; or at least, such evidence shifted the burden of proof to the master to show a subsequent slave maternal ancestor. The presumption of slavery accordingly could be either substantiated or removed by the principle of *partus sequitur ventrem.* The caste was more inclusive than the legal relationship of slavery, so that visibility determined caste and presumed slavery, but the latter presumption might, and sometimes was, defeated in freedom suits. Slavery, then, was the typical, but not the universal, status of members of the subordinate caste. Freedom of course did not remove all caste distinctions—they have yet to be removed—but at least removed *personal* subordination.

The failure of the legal status of slavery and the legal recognition of a servile caste always to coincide was especially noticeable of course in the case of free Negroes. A considerable amount of legislation placed disabilities on free Negroes, regardless of their legal freedom. It was, in other words, *caste* law and not slave law. But there was a further point of nonconformity between the legal definition of slavery and caste visibility. By no means all slaves were *racially* (that is, visibly) Negroes. The usual caste grouping, in legislation, was either "Negroes and mulattoes" or "Negroes and persons of color." But this was scarcely a precise definition, since it left in question the caste (and therefore presumptive legal) status of those with less than one-half of Negro ancestry. More precise definitions varied between states, some adopting definite proportions of Negro ancestry or number of generations removed from a Negro ancestor, and others relying upon judgment from inspection.[30] In no case in the pre-war South was the doctrine maintained that one Negro ancestor or "one drop of Negro blood" was sufficient to place a person in the subordinate caste, and in some cases was definitely denied. This is interesting in view of the fact that one Negro slave ancestor in the maternal line, regardless of union with Whites, was sufficient to establish the legal status of slavery. It was thus possible—and did in fact happen—that persons who were visibly members of the dominant caste could legally be held as slaves. In suits for freedom, however, those persons had an advantage in the legal principle that was a corollary of the presumption of slavery arising from color: the burden of proof of slavery lay on him who held as a slave a person who by "inspection" was visibly White. How this rule was applied by the courts may be illustrated by the report of a Virginia case in 1806.

Per Cur, Tucker, J. All white persons are and ever have been free in this country. If one evidently white be, notwithstanding claimed as a slave, the proof lies on the party claiming to make out the other his slave.

Per Roane, J. In the case of a person visibly appearing to be a negro, the presumption is in this country, that he is a slave, and it is incumbent on him to make out his right to freedom; but in the case of a person visibly appearing to be a white man, or an Indian, the presumption is that he is free, and it is necessary for his adversary to show that he is a slave.

. . . Nature has stamped upon the African and his descendants two characteristic marks, besides the difference of complexion, which often remain visible long after the characteristic distinction of color either disappears or becomes doubtful: a flat nose and woolly head of hair. The latter of these characteristics disappears the last of all. And so strong an ingredient in the African constitution is this latter character, that it predominates uniformly where the party is in equal degree descended from parents of different complexions, whether Whites or Indians, giving to the jet black hair of Indians a degree of flexure which never fails to betray that the party distinguished by it cannot trace his lienage [*sic*] purely from the race of native Americans. Its operation is still more powerful where the mixture happens between persons descended equally from Europeans and African parents . . .

Suppose three persons; a black or mulatto man or woman with a flat nose and woolly head; a copper-colored, with long jetty black straight hair; and one with fair complexion, brown hair, not woolly, or inclining thereto, with a prominent Roman nose, were brought together before a judge on a *habeas corpus,* on the ground of false imprisonment and detention in slavery; that the only evidence the person detaining them in his custody could produce was an authenticated bill of sale from another person, and that the parties themselves were unable to produce any other evidence concerning themselves, whence they came, & c. How must a judge act in such a case? I answer, he must judge from his own view. He must discharge the white person and the Indian out of custody, . . . and he must redeliver the black or mulatto person with the flat nose and the woolly hair to the person claiming to hold him or her as a slave . . . This case may show how far the *onus probandi* may be shifted from one party to the other.[31]

Because of the greater chance of a white slave—not yet used as a synonym for prostitute—establishing his freedom before the courts, and the greater chance of his effective escape, it is quite understandable that in cases involving the evaluation of slave property a white complexion was admitted to decrease the value of the slave.[32]

THE BASIC ISSUE: PERSON OR PROPERTY?

This discussion of the determination of status by caste law and slave law has implied the conception of a legal relationship between persons, or legal groups of persons. But the slave was not uniformly regarded by law as a person. An essential requirement for understanding the relation between the ethical conceptions and convictions concerning slavery, on the one hand, and matters of economic interests, public policy, and private convenience, on the other, is that of the doubtful status of the slave before the law. Was he a person or a piece of property? Legislatures and courts gave no unequivocal answer. The general tenor of legislative definitions of slavery, when such were given at all, was that the slave was property. The most succinct definition was that contained in the Civil Code of Louisiana which says, "A slave is one who is in the power of a master to whom he belongs. The master may sell him, dispose of his person, his industry, and his labor: he can do nothing, possess nothing, nor acquire anything but what must belong to the master." [33] Other laws and court decisions, while less general in their statements, were fully as definite in their declarations that the slave was an object of property. Court decisions in Virginia, Kentucky, and Florida declared the slave to be a chattel.[34] For certain purposes of transfer, by sale or gift, and seizure for debts, slaves were regarded as personal estate.[35] In other cases, such as inheritance of slave property, slaves were regarded as real estate.[36]

Although it is possible to maintain that these legal definitions simply were solutions of the technical problems arising from changes in slave ownership and did not deny the personality of the slave, the denial of the slave as person clearly follows from some other legal principles. One such related principle was that the slave could own nothing.[37] The denial of the right to be the subject of property is a serious limitation of legal personality. In the Roman civil code not only the *peculium* of the slave—what he could earn and save over and above the service required by the master—was recognized, but also rights in possession, although not ownership, of personal effects—the *precarium*.[38] In the South, the slave's possible earnings were given no recognition legally, although cases of self-purchase were not unknown. The self-redemption depended, however, on the generosity of the master, for if the master chose to break his promise to allow it, and appropriated the slave's extra earnings, while retaining him in slavery, the slave had no grounds for legal action.[39] In the case of small amounts of money or personal property, the slave could legally hold no title, since ownership was by law vested in the master. But rights of possession were recognized by the courts.[40] The slave, then, could not be the subject of a property relation, but his limited legal personality might be recognized as the subject of occupancy or possession. Perhaps more significant was the fact that the slave could be a party to no contract, nor to a civil suit. The only suit he could present before the courts was a suit for his freedom. Practice varied concerning the slave's ability to petition for freedom in his own name, or through a "next friend" (*prochain ami*).

The rule regarding the inability of the slave to be a party to a contract was universal in the South,[41] and its implications important. A contractual relationship assumes, at least for the purposes of the contract, an equality of the parties, and a voluntary arrangement. Neither of these criteria could apply to the slave. In short, a contractual system rests upon the ethico-legal conception that individuals are "free moral agents," and enter into contracts for their mutual advantage. Thus, as Durkheim[42] points out, contractual relations take place within established rules. Equality, or at least willingness, of the contracting parties is insured, for example, by the voiding of contracts procured through force or fraud. Moreover, certain contracts which are against public policy are uniformly void. Among such prohibited agreements in civilized societies are those by which a man would sell himself, or others, into slavery.[43]

It is ironic to note that various legislators in the South during the latter part of the slavery period were so insensitive to this point that legislative provision was made for the voluntary enslavement of free Negroes.[44] Clearly, if free Negroes sold themselves into slavery, it would be a Faustian bargain indeed, for once enslaved the recipient of the price would no longer own his purchase price. If the free Negro simply entered slavery for care and feeding, that would speak volumes for the subordinate *caste* status of Negroes such that slavery, with particular responsibility to, and by, a master might be superior to freedom and starvation.

To return to contracts. The slave's legal incompetence to enter into contracts denied that he was a person at least in this sense.

It naturally followed from this inability to be a party to a contract that the slave could not be a party to a civil suit. As Wheeler notes:

Slaves are themselves considered as property, and can neither take, possess, or retain any, except for the use of their masters. A slave cannot be a party to a suit, except in the single case where the negro is held as a slave, and he claims to be free. . . . It would be an idle form and ceremony to make a slave a party to a suit, by the instrumentality of which he could recover nothing; or if recovery could be had, the instant it was recovered would belong to the master. The slave can possess nothing; he can hold nothing. He is, therefore, not a competent party to a suit. And the same rule prevails whereever [*sic*] slavery is tolerated, whether there be legislative enactments upon the subject or not.[45]

Perhaps the most outstanding application of the legal rule that a slave could not be a party to a contract, and certainly the one most often pointed out by the abolitionists, was the denial of any legal marriage, either between slaves, or between a slave and a freeman. This meant, in conjunction with the rule of *partus sequitur ventrem,* that the slave child had no legal father (whether the father was slave or free). It meant also that the child of a free mother by a slave father was *ipso facto* a bastard. The slave "husband" or "wife" might be forced to testify against the other partner in a criminal case (otherwise long exempted in Common Law judicial proceedings). The union between slaves might be as permanent or temporary as the interests of the slaves, or especially of the masters, might dictate. The union was subject at any time to being broken through sale of one of the slaves. Moreover, the charge of adultery could not be made against a slave, and the male slave had no legal action against another, whether slave, free Negro, or White, for intercourse with his "wife," nor could he present such evidence in his defense on a criminal charge of assault and battery or murder. *The slave had no honor to defend.*[46] In this the slave codes of the South went much further than the Roman civil code, where a type of marriage (*contubernium,* not *connubium*) was recognized.[47]

But if for some purposes, and in respect to certain highly significant social relationships, the slave was not regarded as a person, it does not follow that he was uniformly regarded solely as a piece of property. We have noted that in the early development of the legal definitions and conceptions of American Negro slavery the question of conversion and baptism of slaves raised precisely this problem, at least by implication. For there was little denying the fact that the admission of a Negro to the privilege of salvation admitted him thereby, in some sense or other, to the status of a person. (Conversion did not, of course, admit him to *legal* personality, but it may be noted as a general characteristic of the ethical valuation of the person that the personality is not segmented, but treated as a kind of unity. The acceptance of the Negro as a Christian person would and did have at least certain implications concerning legal personality.)

The idea that conversion materially affected (in fact, dissolved) the master-slave relationship died hard. The fact that the earlier question was settled in favor of continued slavery did not dispose conclusively of the related question of the personality of the slave. The persistence of this indeterminacy arising out of religious status must be regarded as at least one source of continued legislative and judicial declarations of the personality of the slave, despite other definitions and implications to the contrary. The ramifications of the problem, and its importance for the whole analysis of the legal status of slavery, will become evident from an examination of situations and relationships that depended upon some kind of an answer to it.

Judicial cases which clearly affirmed that the slave was a person were fairly numerous during the slavery period. Of course, from a common-sense point of view, much of the value of the slave as property arose from the fact that he had characteristic human qualities. One judgment states the point definitely:

The value of slaves depends upon physical strength, upon intellectual capacity, upon mental culture, upon moral worth, as fidelity, honesty, obedience, etc., and upon handicraft skill, in short upon a thousand things; it is only in the wretched market of the mere slave trader, that his value can be rated by pound avordupois [sic].[48]

Other judgments made the affirmation that the slave is a person more explicit:

That a slave is a reasonable creature, or more properly, a human being, is not, I suppose, denied. But it is said, that being property, he is not within the protection of the law, and, therefore, the law requires not the manner of his death; that the owner alone is interested, and the state no more concerned, independently of the acts of the legislature on that subject, than in the death of a horse.

This is an argument, the force of which I cannot feel, and leads to consequences abhorrent to my nature: yet if it be the law of the land, it must be so pronounced. . . .

In establishing slavery . . . the law vested in the master the absolute and uncontrolled right to the services of the slave, and the means of enforcing these services, follow as necessary consequences; nor will the law weigh with the most scrupulous nicety, his acts in relation thereto; but the life of the slave being noways necessary to be placed in the power of the owner for the full enjoyment of his services, the law takes care of that . . .[49]

The Act of 1835, ch. 319, does not exclude slaves . . . it is supposed that the word "persons" is a discriminating term, and excludes them. Several examples were furnished from other Acts of Assembly, but they do not sustain the argument. And if they did . . . how should this court decide, in view of the fact that punishments have been inflicted on slaves, on the authority of other laws, where the word "person" is used . . . ? If that word does not include this class, many judicial murders have been committed in this State . . . Hardship upon the master may be assumed in any case where his slave is taken under the law for punishment, for the benefit of society; but if compensation is not provided, it does not become the court to avert the consequences . . . by arresting judgment . . .[50]

But the exact opposite judgment was held in one case:

However deeply it may be regretted, and whether it be politic or impolitic, a slave by our code, is not treated as a person, but (*negotium*), a thing, as he stood in the civil code of the Roman Empire.[51]

In another case in the courts of the same state (Kentucky) the conception of the slave as a person was reaffirmed. The court decided that

. . . although the law of this state considers slaves as property, yet it recognizes their personal existence, and, to a qualified extent, their natural rights. They may be emancipated by their owners; and must, of course, have a right to seek and enjoy the protection of the law in the establishment of all deeds, or wills, or other legal documents of emancipation; and so far, they must be considered as natural persons, entitled to some legal rights, whenever their owners shall have declared, in a proper manner, that they shall, either *in presenti* or *in futuro,* be free; and, to this extent, the general reason of policy which disables slaves as persons, and subjects them to the condition of mere brute property, does not apply; and the reason ceasing, the law ought also to cease.[52]

In many decisions, like the following one, the inconsistency of the conceptions of the slave as property and as a person came into view:

. . . dollars and cents should not be weighed in the balance with life . . . the rule, of exclusion, because of pecuniary interest, has not been applied to a case like the present, and . . . is not applicable . . . The slave is put on trial as a human being; . . . Is it not inconsistent, in the progress of the trial, to treat him as property, like . . . a horse, in the value of which the owner has a pecuniary interest which makes him incompetent as a witness? [53]

Many of the laws of the so-called "slave codes" did in fact rest upon the implied assumption that the slave was a legal person, at least in the sense and to the extent that he was capable of committing crimes, and could be made to stand trial for his criminal action.[54] The number of judicial cases involving slave crimes was of course very large, but a number of these definitely hinged upon, or at least called forth, the admission that the slave was a person.

. . . it is not true that slaves are only chattels . . . and therefore, it is not true that it is not possible for them to be prisoners . . . the Penal Code . . . has them in contemplation . . . as persons capable of committing crimes and as a . . . consequence . . . as capable of becoming prisoners . . .[55]

However, the limitation to the admission of personality was also not to be denied:

Because they are rational *human beings,* they are capable of committing crimes; and in reference to acts which are crimes, are regarded as *persons*. Because they are slaves, they are . . . incapable of performing civil acts; and in reference to all such, they are *things,* not persons . . .[56]

It is hardly too much to say that the slaves were given at least some of the responsibilities of being persons, and scarcely any of the privileges. The peculiarities of this situation are further illustrated by the fact that slaves were recognized as persons who might run away, or commit capital crimes, but if killed in capture or executed by law, provision was made for reimbursing the master for the loss of his property.[57]

Not only was the slave regarded as a person in that he could be guilty of a crime, but it also became a settled legal principle that a crime could be committed against him. The justification of this principle was, however, by no means constant. In a judgment maintaining that an indictment for an assult upon a slave could be made, the court held, "Slaves are treated in our law as property, and, also, as persons . . ." [58] In a similar case a North Carolina court gave a different and more extended justification:

The question . . . presented to the court, is whether a battery, committed on a slave, no justification, or circumstances attending it being shown, is an indictable offense. . . .

. . . It is . . . objected in this case, that no offence has been committed, and the indictment is not sustainable, because the person assaulted is a slave, who is not protected by the general criminal law of the state; but that, as the property of an individual, the owner may be redressed by a civil action. . . .

The instinct of a slave may be, and generally is, tamed into subservience to his master's will, and from him he receives chastisement, whether it be merited or not, with perfect submission; for he knows the extent of the dominion assumed over him, and that the law ratifies the claim. But when the authority is wantonly usurped by a stranger, nature is disposed to assert her rights, and to prompt the slave to a resistance, often momentarily successful, sometimes fatally so. The public peace is thus broken, as much as if a free man had been beaten, for the party of the aggressor is always the strongest, and such contests usually terminate by overpowering the slave, and inflicting on him a severe chastisement, without regard to the original cause of the conflict. There is, consequently, as much reason for making such offences indictable, as if a white man had been the victim. A wanton injury committed on a slave is a great provocation to the owner, awakens his resentment, and has a direct tendency to a breach of the peace, by inciting him to seek immediate vengeance. . . . Reason and analogy seem to require that a human being, although the subject of property, should be so far protected as the public might be injured through him.

For all purposes necessary to enforce the obedience of the slave, and to render him useful as property, the law secures to the master a complete authority over him, and it will not lightly interfere with the relation thus established. It is a more effectual guarantee of his right of property, when the slave is protected from wanton abuse from those who have no power over him; for it cannot be disputed, that a slave is rendered less capable of performing his master's service, when he finds himself exposed by the law to the capricious violence of every turbulent man in the community.[59]

In general, however, the chief crime that could be committed against a slave was that of homicide,[60] and a master could not be indicted for assault and battery on his own slave. One eloquent decision poignantly notes that

. . . upon the general question, whether the owner is answerable *criminaliter,* for a battery upon his own slave, or other exercise of authority or force, not forbidden by statute, the court entertains but little doubt. That he is so liable, has never been decided; nor, as far as is known, been hitherto contended. There has [sic] been no prosecutions of the sort. . . . The end [of slavery] is the profit of the master, his security and the public safety; the subject, one doomed in his own person, and his posterity, to live without knowledge, and without capacity to make any thing his own, and to toil that another may reap the fruits. What moral considerations shall be addressed to such a being, to convince him what, it is impossible but that the most stupid must feel and know can never be true; that he is thus to labor upon a principle of natural duty, or for the sake of his own personal happiness, such services can only be expected from one who has no will of his own; who surrenders his will in implicit obedience to that of another. Such obedience is the consequence only of uncontrolled authority over the body. There is nothing else which can operate to produce the effect. The power of the master must be absolute, to render the submission of the slave perfect. I most freely confess my sense of the harshness of this proposition. I feel it as deeply as any man can. And as a principle of moral right, every person in his retirement must repudiate it. But in the actual condition of things, it must be so. There is no remedy. This discipline belongs to the state of slavery. They cannot be disunited, without abrogating at once the rights of the master, and absolving the slave from his subjection. It constitutes the curse of slavery to both the bond and the free portions of our population. But it is inherent in the relation of master and slave. . . .

. . . The court . . . disclaims the power of changing the relation in which these parts of our people stand to each other.

. . . The court is compelled to declare, that while slavery exists amongst us in its present state . . . it will be the imperative duty of the judges to recognize the full dominion of the owner over the slave, except where the exercise of it is forbidden by statute. And this we do upon the ground, that this dominion is essential to the value of slaves as property, to the security of the master, and the public tranquility, greatly dependent upon their subordination; and, in fine, as most effectually securing the general protection and comfort of the slaves themselves.[61]

From this general "legal dominion" of the master over the slave a number of other principles followed. One of these was that the master was not held responsible for the death of a slave due to "moderate" correction. In the language of one of the early statutes,

if any slave resist his master (or other by his master's order correcting him) and by the extremity of coercion should chance to die, that his death shall not be accounted felony, but the master . . . be acquitted from molestation, since it cannot be presumed that prepensed malice (which alone makes murder felony) should induce any man to destroy his own estate.[62]

Not only is the confusion between property interests and recognition of legal personality apparent in laws exempting the master from responsibility for death resulting from "moderate" correction, but the definition of the latter must be technical, and not pragmatic. As one abolitionist wrote, with some feeling: "To style the *'correction'* of a slave which causes DEATH, *'moderate,'* is a solecism too monstrous for sober legislation." [63]

In general, more circumstances would extenuate the killing of a slave,[64] and he could uniformly be killed if escaping and showing resistance to capture.[65]

As in the case of the slave's ability to commit a crime, so in the case of the possibility of a crime being committed against him, the question of his status as property or as a person remained indecisive. This becomes particularly apparent from the master's ability to recover damages caused him by an assault or homicide upon his slave by another.

The criminal offense of assault and battery cannot, at common law, be committed on the person of a slave. For notwithstanding for some purposes a slave is regarded in law as a person, yet generally he is a mere chattel personal, and his right of personal protection belongs to his master, who can maintain an action of trespass for the battery of his slave.[66] [Since, at common law, there was no such thing as slavery, the judge can be peremptorily judged a legal idiot.]

The slave, who could be guilty of a crime, and have crimes committed against him, could not be a competent witness to any crime committed by a White. This was supposed to be for reasons of public policy. When his testimony was allowed for or against a free Negro or slave, he was never put under oath as a responsible person.[67]

Through all of the legal principles, enactments, and decisions in justification and definition of the legal status of slavery, there was a deep-seated ambivalence between the conception of the slave as property and as a person. The law seemed to give him recognition as a person with one hand, and to take it away with the other. The slave could be guilty of a crime as a person, but if killed or executed his master might be paid for the loss of his property. An assault upon a slave by an unauthorized person was judged to be a criminal offense, but this was in the interest of keeping the peace, and the master could maintain a suit for damage to his property. The crime of murder could be committed against a slave, but ordinarily not by his master, since the latter would scarcely plan to destroy his property.

The chief value of the slave as property lay in his being a person, but his chief value as a person lay in his being held as property.

This total ambivalence must certainly be regarded as significant in the always-partial institutionalization of the slavery system. The economic relationships of slavery had to be placed within a wider institutional framework, and that framework included the common claims of humanity—underscored both by the Common Law, whereby the rights of Englishmen had become the rights of man, but also by the essentially equalitarian sentiments which underlay part of the ideology of the American Revolution.

The courts in Southern jurisdictions were (and have remained) rather "strict constructionists" in terms of legal precedent. The law of slavery, which was legislative law and not judicial law, was totally antithetical to the law as developed in cases (in shorthand terms, the Common Law). We thus encounter the conspicuous squirming of judges rendering decisions on cases involving slaves and slavery. But, more ironically, we encounter judges who would, by contemporary judgment, be regarded as the most conservative having the greatest difficulty in dealing with what was essentially an alien institution. A patina of legal precedent was occasionally adduced by reference to the Roman law of slavery (essentially the Justinian Code), but even a badly trained jurist had to know that the Roman law had had *no* binding effect on English or American law after the English Reformation. No, the judges suffered, and squirmed, and generally upheld the legislative acts that supported an evil system, but a system that was in the interests of the judges' "own kind." One may, at more than a century's distance, suffer a bit for the dilemma of the judges. But only a little.

V

Social Structure
and the Defense
of Slavery

American Negro slavery as a labor system, which increasingly became tied to an economic system of monoculture for the production of commercial crops, was never untainted by mere considerations of conspicuous display. The careful calculus of slave management produced relatively dispassionate articles in *De Bow's Review,* worthy of a later technical literature on agronomy and animal husbandry. Yet the ethical position of slavery was never secure, and, ironically, especially with respect to slaves that were more nearly owned servants for the affluent than mere farm animals, for the servant was of small use unless he possessed human qualities.

The personality of the slave inevitably became a legal issue in both civil and criminal matters, and that issue also was never successfully resolved. The dilemma was intrinsic, and necessarily became deeper and more poignant whenever the distinctly human qualities of the slave were of paramount importance.

Thus it would be quite improper to consider slavery as adequately described by economics and law, or even to think of the economic and legal aspects of the slavery system as always more "primary" or "basic" than other aspects. Slavery involved much more than these. It consisted of a network of social relationships highly structured and institutionalized at the one extreme, highly irregular at the other; a focus of class alignments, and central to a caste system; a "peculiar institution" defended by reference to everything from unfortunate necessity to the will of God; a legitimized exploitation of a "docile" and "stupid" type of sub-humans, who yet persisted in trying to acquire the success goals of the exploiters, and of whom the dominant caste stood in almost constant fear.

It is not always easy to untangle the principal elements in so complex, and by no means neatly organized, a social system. It may therefore be most satisfactory to start with an analysis of the institutional and organizational features of the master-slave relationship, and proceed to the class and caste structure, and finally to the attempted justification of slavery in theory and sentiment.

THE MASTER-SLAVE RELATIONSHIP

Since slavery was, among other things, the labor system employed in a highly competitive market economy, a minimum of rational efficiency was necessarily prescribed for economic survival. Yet there was a strong element of approved traditionalism bound up with the idealization of the patriarchal organization of plantation life and the maintenance of the family estate and family slaves at all costs. George Washington, one of the most prosperous of the colonial planters, and by no means an easy or "sentimental" master, retained his slaves when clearly unprofitable because he was "principled against selling negroes." [1]

The institutions surrounding the slavery relationship not only served to provide the framework for an economic system, but also had to function on a wider basis in reference to a series of more or less related problems of social control. Although slavery involved a legitimization of labor exploitation, there were definite institutional limitations on that exploitation at the point (obviously not very definite) where emphasis upon productive efficiency entailed serious departure from the traditional "gentlemanly" conduct of the planter aristocracy. D. R. Hundley, an able contemporary observer who wrote in defense of that aristocracy, devotes a full chapter to a condemnatory description of the "Southern Yankee." [2] Part of his condemnation brings out clearly the disapproval of thorough-going economic rationality:

In the tobacco-fields of Virginia, in the rice-fields of Carolina, in the cotton-fields of Alabama, or among the sugar-canes of Louisiana, when a farmer or planter, he [the "Southern Yankee"] is in all things similar and equally bent on the accumulation of the sordid pelf: and the crack of the whip is heard early, and the crack of the same is heard late, and the weary backs of his bondmen and bondwomen are bowed to the ground with over-tasking and over-toil, and yet his heart is still unsatisfied; for he grasps after more and more, and cries to the fainting slave: "Another pound of money, dog, or I take a pound of flesh!" And the lash is never staid, save by one single consideration only—will it pay? [3]

The defense of slavery in comparison with the exploitative "wage slavery" of the industrial North also was characterized by an emphasis upon traditionalistic factors involved in the relationship of the planter and his servants in comparison with the sheerly economic relationship of employer and employee. [4] The notable departures from this institutional norm are no denial of its existence, but only indicative of an instability in the social organization to which it applied.

Legally, the domination and authority of the master were fairly complete. This legitimate power was given general approval, and laxity in maintaining that authority was condemned. The legitimate use of physical coercion was an important factor in the approved master-slave relationship, but the sole or principal reliance upon such a basis of dominance and authority implied a "truncated" institutional order. That is, the physical coercion might be, and was, approved by the "effective community"—those of the dominant caste—but for a given master-slave relationship of that kind it amounted to a denial of the acceptance by the slave of the legitimacy of the master's authority. In short, if the slave did not work willingly and meekly, he was not a party to, or supporter of, the institutional order which fixed his status, and the duties proper to it. However, there is slight reason to believe that the use of the whip was sheerly coercive. There is evidence that the legitimacy of physical punishment by the master or others in a position of dominance over the slave was at least partially accepted by the slave. In other words, the use of the whip was a badge of authority, but not the sole, or perhaps even primary, means of obtaining and maintaining that authority. Phillips, a latter-day apologist for the slavery system, indicates that physical violence upon the slave was almost universal in the master-slave relationship.[5]

The abolitionists made a great deal of the point, apparently fairly well established, that a great deal of the physical violence of the master or overseer upon the slave had no immediate end, such as coercion to labor or "correction" of shortcomings, but was simply a general symbol of legitimate authority. We have observed that the absence of any immediate "justification" of violence upon a slave was no legal argument against its legitimacy. Although the incidence of cruelties to slaves cannot be determined, the resort to severe physical violence was at least not uncommon. Theodore Weld, one of the leading abolitionists, collected (and selected) evidence of such violence chiefly from Southern sources. In his *American Slavery as It Is: Testimony of a Thousand Witnesses,*[6] he presented evidence of whipping scars, gunshot wounds, and a variety of physical mutilations, quoted from advertisements in Southern newspapers. The following are typical samples:

WITNESSES	TESTIMONY
Mr. Robert Nicoll, Dauphin st. between Emmanuel and Concep-	"Ten dollars reward for my woman Siby, *very much scarred about the*

WITNESSES

TESTIMONY

tion st's. Mobile, Alabama, in the "Mobile Commercial Advertiser."

neck and ears by whipping."

Mr. Cornelius D. Tolin, Augusta, Ga., in the "Chronicle and Sentinel," Oct. 18, 1838.

"Ranaway, a negro man named Johnson— he has a *great many marks of the whip* on his back."

Mr. John Wotton, Rockville Montgomery county, Maryland, in the "Baltimore Republican," Jan. 13, 1838.

"Ranaway, Bill—has *several* LARGE SCARS on his back from a *severe* whipping in *early* life."

James Dorrah, Deputy sheriff, Claiborne county, Mi., in the "Port Gibson Correspondent," April 15, 1837.

"Committed to jail, negro man Toy—he has been *badly whipped."*

M. Gridly, sheriff of Adams county, Mi., in the "Memphis (Tenn.) Times," September, 1834.

"Was committed to jail, a Negro boy—had on a *large neck iron* with a *huge pair of horns and a large bar or band of iron* on his left leg."

Mr. Micajah Ricks, Nash County, North Carolina, in the Raleigh "Standard," July 18, 1838.

"Ranaway, a negro woman and two children: a few days before she set off, *I burnt her with a hot iron,* on the left side of her face, *I tried to make the letter* M."

Mr. J. Biship, Bishopville, Sumpter District, South Carolina, in the "Camden [S. C.] Jour-

"Ranaway a negro named Arthur, has a considerable *scar* across his *breast* and each *arm*

WITNESSES	TESTIMONY
nal," March 4, 1837.	made by a knife; loves to talk much of the goodness of God."
Mr. J. P. Ashford, Adams Co. Mi. in the "Natchez Courier," August 24, 1838.	"Ranaway a negro girl called Mary, has a small scar over her eye, a *good many teeth missing,* the letter **A** is *branded on her cheek and forehead.*"
J. L. Jolley, Sheriff of Clinton Co. Mi., in the "Clinton Gazette," July 23, 1836.	"Was committed to jail a negro man, says his name is Josiah, his back very much scarred by the whip, and *branded on the thigh and hips,* in three or four places, thus (J. M.) the *rim of his right ear has been bit or cut off.*"
Mr. Littlejohn Hynes, Hinds Co. Mi. in the "Natchez Courier," August 17, 1836.	"Ranaway, a negro named Jerry, has a small piece *cut out of the top of each ear.*" [7]

Even if it were possible to examine all such advertisements of and for runaway slaves, the typicality of physical mutilations resulting from violence could by no means be established. These slaves were fugitives from labor, in itself an indication that the cases are selected from among those who had not passively accepted the slavery relationship. Moreover, it would obviously be the practice whether of the masters of runaways or of law officers who had detained fugitives to indicate distinguishing characteristics to aid in identification. All such evidence can establish is that there were some slaves who bore marks of physical violence and this evidence could be interpreted as cruel treatment.

The dominance and authority of the master, though always rest-ing upon the possibility of physical coercion, was insured by other institutionally prescribed behavior. Perhaps most significant were the expected actions on the part of the slave indicating deference to and acceptance of authority. Many of these became definitely ritualistic, and indicated an outward conformity to a status situation. Thus, the Negro could never remain seated in the presence of a White person; a male slave removed his hat while talking to any one in a position of authority; if he wore no hat he tugged deferentially at his forelock; he was expected to give assent to all suggestions and opinions of the master.[8] Terms of reference and address were also of ritual and symbolic importance in respect to deference and authority. The terms of reference and address used by the slave varied from those of formal respect, such as "Sir," to those of informal deference, such as "Massa," "Mars," "Miss," "Missy." The Negro slave might be addressed by his given name (he ordinarily had no other), if known, or as "boy," or the even more derogatory term, "nigger" (according to Hundley, not used by Southern "gentlemen"[9]). Reference to Negro slaves included all of these forms, and also stereotyped and depersonalized terms as "buck," "hand," "black fellow," "female," and "wench." "Negro" was not spelled with a capital "N." There was no uncertainty among Southern slaveholders concerning the propriety of the dominance and authority of the master and the subservience of the slave, but there remained the related question of the specific forms that this status relationship should take. Although physical coercion as a basis for a purely compulsory social relationship was possible and sanctioned, the slave was also expected to accept his position and to behave accordingly by being obsequious and deferential.

In a competitive market economy such as that in which the plantation-slavery system developed, rational economic self-interest would seem to be expected as an institutional characteristic. Yet in the labor system, we have been saying, there was a strong element of approved traditionalism. The plantation-slavery system was a commercial enterprise, but also a general social system of differential rights and duties, privileges and responsibilities. The emphasis on rational self-interest on the one hand or traditional-istic norm on the other hand varied in the South in both time and space. This variation has been summarized by Gray:

Generally speaking, on the larger plantations the life of the slave was more nearly ordered by rule. His labor was more regular but also frequently more severe, although qualifications must be applied according to section and region. It was observed about 1837 that the subdivision of plantations which resulted from the changes in laws of inheritance had made for a milder treatment of slaves. On large plantations provision for the physical well-being of the slave was more likely to be reduced to rule and ad-justed to teachings of experience. Large plantations, however, were more capitalistic and commercial than were many of the smaller slave properties, and the pressure of credit obligations frequently was responsible for relatively harder driving. Furthermore, on large plantations slaves were likely to be subject to the overseer system, which was conducive to hard driving and poor treatment. The operation of estates by tenants for life, relatively frequent in the colonial period, also made for harsh treatment. On the small plantations and farms there was a closer personal relation between master and slave, with all the mitigations made possible by ability to depart from fixed rule and to employ that mode of treatment best adapted to the individual case. Absentee ownership and the resulting evils of the overseer system were less prevalent. The slave shared the prosperity and adversity of the Master. The latter was likely to speak of his slave force as his "family" and to feel the responsibility growing out of such an attitude. There were many large plantations also, especially in the older plantation regions, where masters were dominated by a similar sense of obligation. Frequently the women of the planter's family assumed a heavy load of responsibility in providing clothing, nursing the sick, and caring for the aged and children. . . .

In regions where the numerical preponderance of Negroes was large, the sense of insecurity resulted in greater severity. For this reason the treatment of slaves was in general more severe in South Carolina and Georgia than in Virginia and Maryland. Similarly, in the newer districts of the Southwest, where the supply of slaves had largely been obtained by recent purchase, there was a general absence of personal attachments between master and slaves. Masters were also less subject to the restraining influence of public opinion, for social relations were less firmly established. Moreover, the planting class contained a larger proportion of the newly rich, a class largely responsible for the observation that Northern overseers and foreign owners made the hardest masters.[10]

The plantation system, we have noted, tended during the latter part of the slavery period to approach the ideal type of a purely commercial economic organization, and this tendency was associated with the geographical shift to the new lands of the Southwest. It was during the latter part of the slavery period, then, and as a concomitant of increased economic efficiency that the master-slave relationship became one of rational self-interest on the part of the master (to whom a field hand might be entirely unknown), and a tendency to rely to a greater extent upon the self-interest of the slave. That is, in so far as the labor of the slave was that of an economic unit, and secured in the first instance by physical coercion, or the threat of it, willing and disinterested service of the slave was not expected. Given the control and possible physical coercion by the master or his representative, it might be, and undoubtedly often was, a situation so structured that the slave was expected to act only in conformity with self-interest: obey to escape the lash. This situation was apparently the basis for the fear among the slaves of Virginia and Maryland, and later of the entire Eastern cotton belt, of being "sold down the river." [11]

The variation between rationality and traditionalism, between the type of superiority and inferiority based upon pure compulsion and the type entailing legitimized deference and accepted authority, must make it clear that the institutional variation was between divergent composite types of the master-slave relationship. That is, rationality, pure compulsion, and self-interest are to be contrasted with the equally approved traditionalism accompanied by deference and accepted authority. This indefiniteness of the institutional order becomes even more pronounced if other possible modes of variation are considered. That is, associated with the first composite type were ethical universalism, functional specificity, and impersonality.[12] The second type of relationship was characterized by ethical particularism, functional diffuseness, and affectivity. How these modes of institutional variation were related may appear from a further examination of the divergent types already noted.

The polar type of master-slave relationship which has been characterized by the expression "sheerly economic," and which was very nearly approached in the large plantations of the Southwest, depended upon ethical universalism. That is, within the framework of the slavery system the relation between any given master and any given slave depended upon no previous relationships. Authority and rules applied to the slave as a slave, and not as any particular person. This is associated with the process of categorization, for it obviated the necessity of dealing with individual persons as such. This might, and the abolitionists claim did, mean that a master would freely exploit, coerce, and sell his own children by one of his female slaves. Their status as slaves took precedence over their biological relation to the master, for they did not institutionally belong to the kinship organization of the father, which would give them claim to preferential treatment.

Likewise, in this polar type of relationship, functional specificity was characteristic. That is, the sole nexus was that of the profit of the master from the labor of the slave, and of the satisfaction by the slave of the work demands made upon him. The relationship of master and slave was thus impersonal; the emotional adherence to the organizational situation was not problematical. This polar type of master-slave relationship has been aptly summarized by Sorokin:

A slave to a cruel master is but a mere instrument, something even more "unhuman" than his cattle; at best, he is but a species of animal . . . the coercing party remains . . . a stranger to the coerced. It is felt and perceived not as a human personality capable of understanding, feeling, being united by a psychological *rapport;* it is perceived merely as an instrument of oppression—cruel, inhuman, perverse, unjust, a kind of "whip" which only hurts, tortures, oppresses. There is no bridge of real mutual understanding between the parties as human beings and personalities; there is no mutual fusion and no "we" feeling except the purely external, mechanical, like that between a cruel driver and his horse. The inner world of each party is mutually closed to the other; often there is not even the desire to open it.[13]

The other clear type of master-slave relationship, which approached the "familistic," [14] introduced elements of particularity. That is, the master regarded his labor force as in some sense part of his family. The relationship was therefore not one between representatives of social categories, within which individual differences were irrelevant, but one between a particular master and a particular laborer who secondarily belonged to the general category of Negro slaves.[15] Likewise, the rights and obligations of the master and slave were by no means limited in function to the economic nexus, but included a wide variety of rights and duties unspecified in advance. Wider interests were not only legitimate but in a general sense expected. The slave was expected not only to serve his master at specified tasks, but to aid in case of any unforseen contingency arising. Moreover, he was expected not only to serve his master, but to love him. The master also was not limited by his economic interest in the slave, but regarded his obligations as more far-reaching, including the slave's comfort, security in old age, religious welfare, and so on. He might form strong emotional attachments to slaves, and it was quite proper for him to do so. Affectivity, not impersonality, was the order.

The institutional order within which masters and slaves interacted and carried on social relationships was thus by no means determinate. Two distinct "ideal types" have here been distinguished, and of course on the concrete level there were wide variations and combinations between these two types.

Now if it be granted for the moment, in view of the evidence garnered from the analysis of the legal status of slavery, and pending further evidence to be presented in this chapter, that a significant element of the general value system of the South was an ethical valuation of the individual, the polar types of master-slave relationship here discussed may be viewed as they relate to that value or culture goal. It may then be suggested that one method of relating the slavery system to the diffuse culture goal of valuation of the individual was that of personalizing, particularizing, diffusing, and traditionalizing the master-slave relationship. This type of solution, however, had its disadvantages, since the slave remained officially, and to a significant degree actually, a slave; he might be recognized and valued as an individual, and his capabilities partially developed, but this might and did run counter to the stability of the slavery system. Hundley, who idealized the familistic type of slavery system, still noted with disapproval the tendency to undue liberality of treatment, and especially over-familiarity with the masters. These slaves grew up "to be sleek, and saucy, and rascally." [16] The intrusion of personality considerations into a relationship which was legally a categorized and stereotyped one, was a constant source of difficulty, although widely approved as a defensible type of relationship.[17] Historians have noted the much greater laxity in actual master-slave relationships than might be expected from the slave codes.[18] This may be taken as at least partially satisfactory evidence of the intrusion on the level of social action of the valuation of the individual and a resulting modification in the depersonalized relationship between social categories.

On the other hand, it was possible so to establish the institutional order underlying the master-slave relationship that only the social category of slaves was relevant, and the question of the valuation of the individual slave was unproblematical. This appears to have been true of the polar type of sheerly economic organization. Robert E. Park has suggested in this connection that the function of the cynicism of the overseer and slave trader (both of whom, it will later be noted, were type representatives of the exclusively economic structure) was "a sort of protective device, the function of which is to make men immune to the sentiments which the conditions of persons with whom they are associated would naturally inspire." [19] It may be suggested that the sentiments would be "naturally inspired" only in view of a more general, if diffuse, value in the society attaching to the individual. Much of the Southern defense of slavery was in terms of the familistic type, which seemed to concede that humanity.

THE BROADER SYSTEM OF INEQUALITY

The significance of the slavery system for the social structure of the ante-bellum South was not confined to the institutionalization of the master-slave relationship. For the slavery system was in many respects a point of orientation for the entire social organization of Southern society. Despite the general impression to the contrary, slaveholding was in no statistical sense typical of Southern Whites. For the Southern states as a whole, during the period for which census data are available, the percentage of the total free population of those who were slaveholders and their families was only 35.3 in 1790 and declined to 26.1 in 1860.[20] All of those immediately connected with the slavery system (combined slave and slaveholding population) formed only 57 per cent of the entire population in 1790, and precisely one-half in 1860.[21]

The significance of the plantation organization, and of the slavery system generally, was, however, not dependent solely upon numerical weight in the population.

To a very large degree, class status among the White population was determined by the nature of the relation to the slavery system. Among slaveholders, status was largely relative to the number of slaves held. Among non-slaveholders, the immediacy of relationship or closeness of approximation to the goal of slaveholding was the primary relevant consideration.

Any division of members of a social system is likely to be arbitrary in some degree and no single criterion, even, as in this case, the relation to the slavery system, will be entirely satisfactory. Still, a rough but significant approximation is possible. At the top in the social stratification among the Whites was the "aristocracy." Although various types have been distinguished within this group, and somewhat legitimately, economic success, chiefly as symbolized by ownership of a large number of slaves, was of primary importance for membership. It is true that in the older plantation regions there was associated with the aristocracy of wealth a strong tendency to base membership upon family connections and traditions. This seems to be the chief basis for Hundley's distinction between "Southern Gentlemen" and "Cotton Snobs." [22] Gray distinguishes the "aristocracy" and the "plutocratic planters," but notes that the former class was chiefly removed from the category of the latter by mere lapse of time.[23] The distinction is, of course, closely associated with the polar types of master-slave relationship previously discussed, since the "true" aristocracy was associated with the familistic type of relationship, whereas the "plutocracy" was associated with the sheerly economic type of organization. Shugg notes the almost exclusively monetary basis of upper class membership in Louisiana.[24] A third group should be included in the aristocracy, because of their close relationship with the large planters and dependence upon their dominance for social status. This group included the wealthy urban "factors" and merchants, and the learned professions.

Just below the various groups included in the aristocracy, and at times separable from them only by arbitrary divisions, were those making up the upper middle class. These included small planters, commercial farmers, lesser merchants, and some professionals. Although representing a variety of occupational interests, not too neatly comparable, and a fairly wide range of economic well-being, all were more or less closely allied with the slavery system, and dependent upon it to an appreciable degree for their social position. Because of their position as slaveholders, or their close relationship with slaveholders and general acceptance as social equals, their interests and class affiliations more nearly approached those of the aristocracy than those below them in the scheme of stratification.

Despite the aristocratic tradition, those of the upper middle class were valued members of Southern society.

Slightly lower in the scale of stratification than those of the upper middle class, but partially merging into it, were the independent non-slaveholding farmers (yeomen), who were not to be accounted equals of the slaveholding classes, but yet remained respectable and respected members of the community. Also members of what may be called the lower middle class were independent White artisans, and, to a certain extent, the independent "highlanders" who were separated from the slavery system spatially as well as economically.[25]

In an anomalous position in the class structure were those two necessary but overtly despised groups, whose social status was not commensurate with their economic standing: the slave-traders and the overseers. The former group was avowedly universally despised by defenders of the slavery system. Yet they served a necessary function in moving slaves from places where they were in excess supply to where they were scarce, and as agents in maintaining the fluidity of the slave market. A number of "reasons" for despisal of slave-traders were usually given, chiefly in terms of undesirable traits of character. All were supposed to be dishonest, unscrupulous, greedy, ill-bred, and immoral.[26] Bancroft has shown that this was by no means generally true but that the stereotype remained.[27] It may be suggested that there was a value conflict involved in fixing the status of the trader.

The almost universal deprecation of the slave trade throughout the South, the prevailing hatred of slave traders, as well as numerous efforts to mitigate the hardships of the trade and to prevent separation of kindred are evidences that the trade was felt to be a sore spot in the "peculiar institution." [28]

Although it may be said cynically that the slave-trader bought and sold slaves, and slaveholders sold and bought them, the latter could "justify" his buying and selling in terms of hard necessity, reuniting slave families, or disposing of an unmanageable slave. The trader was openly concerned only with the market. The function performed by the trader as a scapegoat for various guilt feelings concerning the slavery system should not be overlooked.

Analogous in many respects to the slave-trader was the overseer. Like the trader, the overseer's connection with slavery was by virtue of his position primarily or exclusively an economic one. He was hired and fired according to his economic efficiency, as judged primarily by his ability to direct the labor force in the production of a satisfactory profit for the slaveholder. He it was who had the chief immediate responsibility for the sheerly exploitative aspects of the use of slave labor.

At the very bottom of the social scale of the dominant caste were the "poor whites," a narrower term than non-slaveholding Whites. The "poor whites" were not a large group numerically, and were largely separated from the plantation-slavery system geographically. They were to be found on the unproductive lands of the "pine barrens," and were generally accounted as lazy, shiftless, and degenerate. Afflicted with disease arising from poverty, they were known variously as "crackers," "clay-eaters," and "dirt-eaters." [29] Since this lowest White class was of particular significance in relation to slavery and the caste system, and in many respects may serve as a basis for discussing the position of non-slaveholding Whites in general, fuller discussion of the "poor whites" may be deferred momentarily while attention is shifted to the other side of the picture: the Negro.

Between the Whites and Negroes there was truly a great gulf fixed. That gulf consisted in the "caste line." The dominance of the Whites did not rest solely on their legal ownership of slaves, for not all Whites, or even a majority, were slaveholders. Likewise, the subservience of the Negro was not exclusively and immediately due to the slavery relationship, for although a majority of Negroes were slaves, many were freemen. We have seen that Negroes were not only subject to slave law, but also to "caste law"—that is, special disabilities attaching to them as Negroes, regardless of their legal status as slaves or freemen. The caste relationship then was wider than the slavery relationship, and thus the features of caste were not exclusively dependent upon the status of slavery.[30]

Although the possiblity or impossibility of legitimate intermarriage is probably crucial in a caste system, other elements that distinguish it from other types of social stratification may be noted. In a caste system the criteria of membership are clear-cut and rigorously defined. This membership is determined by birth, and this may be the explanation for the prohibition upon caste intermarriage. That is, socially sanctioned marriage normally implies the subsequent class equality of the marriage partners, and the legitimization of the offspring. Without the marriage, the caste status of the child would be indeterminate. This, of course, does not carry over to the inter-caste sexual unions, since these remain unofficial and imply no further social bonds. Moreover, the children of such unions are by definition illegitimate, and can lay no claim to higher caste status than that of the parent belonging to the lower caste. In the Negro-White caste system, as previously noted, this general rule was related to the legal rule concerning the hereditary character of slavery—the child followed the condition of the mother. The usual inter-caste union was between the White male and the Negro female. How extensive such unions were during the slavery period is difficult to determine, but the fairly large number of "Negroes" who were Mulattoes and lighter testifies that they were not rare.[31] The sexual exploitation of female slaves and other Negroes by masters or members of the dominant caste was a further symbol of at least semi-legitimate authority.

In a caste structure individual qualities, worth, achievement, and so on, are irrelevant to caste status. Bond or free, the Negro was subordinate. Since this is social categorization *par excellence* there must be some external symbol for fixing the caste status of any individual whose social background is unknown. Of basic importance in maintaining a caste system is reliable knowledge of parentage in a society marked by limited migration, or high *visibility*. The importance of the visibility of the Negro in establishing the slavery regime has been earlier noted. The presumption of occupational status (slavery) arising from the skin color has also been discussed as basic to the legal conception of slavery. Although this criterion of visibility would not seem to apply in the caste system of India, often taken as a type case, the "visibility" is none the less real, but of a slightly different sort. The Indian caste system is primarily a social structure oriented around relatively immobile village communities where the caste status is known, because the caste of the parents is known.[32] There is, moreover, claimed evidence of at least a rough color gradation from the upper to the lower castes,[33] though that is uncertain and not crucial to the maintenance of the system.

It is only in reference to the caste system, and the barrier of the "color" (or caste) line that the legal and more informal disabilities placed upon free Negroes can be understood. As Craven writes:

Nor should slavery be held responsible for all the harsh regulations made against the Negro's freedom of action. Most of them arose from the fact that he was a *Negro*. A race question was involved.[34]

In general, therefore, the Negro belonged to an inferior caste (demonstrated by his complexion, and enforced by law and custom), and then might or might not be a slave. Although the caste system was in general more inclusive than the slavery system, it was in some cases slightly less inclusive. Those cases were the slaves who were visibly White by inspection, and had the presumption of freedom in their favor because of that fact. Without attempting to distinguish gradations of slaves, the following diagrammatic representation illustrates the relationship between class, legal, and caste lines.[35]

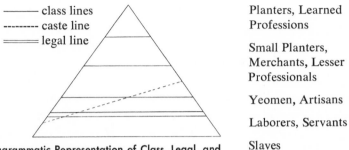

——— class lines
--------- caste line
===== legal line

Planters, Learned
Professions

Small Planters,
Merchants, Lesser
Professionals

Yeomen, Artisans

Laborers, Servants

Diagrammatic Representation of Class, Legal, and   Slaves
Caste Lines in the Ante-Bellum South.

Below the caste line there was only slightly less variability than above it. The free Negroes varied in occupation and economic well-being from fairly prosperous artisans and independent farmers to a status equivalent (except for the caste line) to the poorest of the poor Whites. Below the legal line gradations did not end, for there were social classes or at least marked inequality among the slaves.

Those at the "top of the bottom" in the Southern social structure —the free Negroes—were generally conceded to be a serious problem in the maintenance of that structure. The reasons given for this situation were ordinarily in terms of their sympathy for the slaves, the likelihood of their inciting revolts, and their economic inadequacy. The free Negro was not allowed to vote, was subject along with slaves to the severity of the slave codes, and was considered a constant menace to the slavery system. Toward the end of the slavery period it was almost impossible to emancipate slaves by will, deed of gift, or any other common method; *manumission required a special act of the state legislature.* The available evidence by no means bears out the contention that free Negroes in general actively interfered with the slavery system, or became any greater burden on the community than other classes with limited economic opportunities. Why then fear the free Negro and prohibit the manumission of slaves? As Dumond has remarked, "The mere act of emancipation was looked upon as an implied censure of slavery . . ." [36] Likewise, whatever the "real" danger of free Negroes in the population, their "symbolic" danger cannot be denied. The whole tenor of the development of the legal status of slavery, it has been observed, was to attempt to fix slavery as a status properly attaching to Negroes. In other words, the racial justification of slavery, and the doctrine of presumptive slavery arising from color, may be said to have been an attempt to make the caste line and the slavery line parallel, if not indistinguishable, for those of the subordinate group. The mere presence of free Negroes was a denial that slavery followed naturally and inevitably from Negro ancestry. The manumission of Negroes, moreover, was a notable example of the intrusion of personalistic factors into a stereotyped and categorized situation. It was evidence of the possibility of an extension downward in a diluted form of the values of the dominant caste in respect to individual achievement and the value of liberty, and an indication of some possibility of the slave's legitimately aspiring to those goals.

Below the free Negroes in the scale of stratification were the majority of the Black population, the slaves. The latter might, however, be superior in economic position to the former, since slaves had a fairly large degree of economic security, and varying degrees of comfort. The "freedom" of the free Negro was so little greater than that of the slaves, that it may often have been a poor bargain. Especially was this the case in the later slavery period with the increasing restrictions upon free Negroes and the prevalence of caste, rather than slave, law. Near the end of the slavery period a number of states passed enabling acts to allow free Negroes voluntarily to enter slavery. There is no evidence, however, of any considerable movement to trade even so limited (but official) liberty for slavery.

Slaves were by no means without substantial distinctions. The most clear-cut of these was that between house servants and field hands. Of those Gray writes:

The condition of house servants on large plantations was in marked contrast to that of field servants. The former were in close association with members of the master's family, shared their joys and sorrows, identified themselves with their prosperity and reputation. They enjoyed the first fruits of generosity; theirs was the cast-off clothing and the presents that good form required the visitor to make to servants of his host. They shared in the abundance and variety of the master's table. In many cases their cabins were more commodious than those of field hands and sometimes located in a separate quarter. Together with drivers and the better class of artisans, house servants were the slave aristocracy.[37]

Class distinctions might be multiplied beyond that between house servants and field hands, but with less certainty. Within the general slavery system the status of slaves was partially determined by their occupational rank, but also by a sort of reflected status according to the social class of the master. The relation of slaves to the slavery system was thus by no means identical, and their interest in its preservation or abolition not necessarily so.

THE TRUNCATED SYSTEM: SLAVE DISCONTENT

Previous sections of this chapter have been devoted to the problems associated with the institutionalization of slavery, chiefly in reference to the types of relationship approved by the effective community (the dominant caste). However, as already indicated, the institutionalization of slavery on the basis of dominant caste approval, even if clear-cut, is at best a truncated institutional relationship if not accepted by the slaves. The extent of acceptance by the slaves of the legitimacy of the slavery system cannot be determined precisely, but certain types of evidence and lines of analysis may be examined.

The existence of "social classes" among the slaves, especially distinctions based upon nearness to or distance from the slaveholder and his family, suggests a differential participation in, and acceptance of, the social life of the whites. Of all categories of slaves, probably the house servants and the artisans among town slaves had the greatest opportunity to assimilate the value system of the masters. But the values assimilated might be of two sorts, quite distinct in their implications for acceptance of the slavery system. On the one hand, the slaves might accept the value system in justification of slavery and thereby share in its institutional support. This acceptance, coupled with the prestige and relatively high status afforded the more privileged among the slaves by the slavery system itself might be expected to provide a strong element of stability in the master-slave relationship. On the other hand, the slaves might accept the values held among the Whites in regard to liberty, individual worth, and the like, as legitimate social values and thus interpret their status as illegitimate and unjust. The field hands, although having much less opportunity to assimilate any of the value-attitudes or culture goals of White society, also had fewer immediate and obvious advantages in maintaining their status as slaves.

The slaves have been supposed to be docile, contented, and well adjusted to the slavery system. Phillips speaks of slaves on the plantations as docile, stupid, having occasional grievances but no ambitions.[38] Hundley claimed that slaves were in general contented, and explained that fugitives were low-class, vicious Negroes.[39] Doyle gives great weight to the ceremony and ritual characteristic of inter-caste etiquette as evidence of the slave seeing himself "through his master's eyes." [40]

However, a number of types of evidence point to serious limitations on the picture of docility and acceptance of the institutional order. Negroes imported directly from Africa to the American colonies were not uniformly "tractable," and did not always accept their lot easily. Traders early learned to distinguish various types of African natives according to their tribes or regional dispersion. Some were found easier to "season" than others; some had a propensity for suicide, others for blind rebellion.[41] These individuals, however, were not born into slavery or at least not into the American slavery system, and can scarcely be considered evidence against the general acceptance of slavery by American-born Negroes. An obvious indication of a more or less common discontent and the non-acceptance of the slavery system is to be found in the number of runaways. Although it is impossible from available evidence to construct a statistical measure of the proportion of slaves who ran away from their masters or overseers, the volume of advertising in Southern newspapers supplied by masters offering rewards for the capture of their fugitive slaves and by peace officers announcing detention of runaways is ample testimony that running away was not a rare event.[42]

Escape was not the only resort of discontented slaves. Revolts and insurrections, though seldom of widespread seriousness—due at least in part to isolation of the plantations—were more numerous than has been commonly supposed, and at times gained wide attention causing fairly general alarm. The Nat Turner rebellion, the Denmark Vesey rebellion, and John Brown's *tour de force* at Harper's Ferry are probably the best known. Others, however, dotted the entire history of the American slavery system. Aptheker has reported well over two hundred plots and revolts in the English colonies and in the Southern states from 1663 to 1860.[43] The number of revolts, although not evidence of a universal dissatisfaction with the slavery system, must at least modify the judgment that institutional support of that system was given without reservation by those at the bottom of the social structure.

Another fruitful source of evidence that the slavery system was very imperfectly institutionalized, and was so considered by the dominant caste, is that revealed in the "slave codes." In addition to the laws requiring males to serve on night patrols, and giving these patrols wide powers in the exercise of physical coercion upon slaves abroad at night without passes, a variety of other restrictions upon the slave, and often the entire Negro, population reveal the feeling of insecurity among the Whites. Some of the types of legislation may be reviewed to find the restrictions considered necessary to keep the slave, and lower caste, population in check. There were twenty-one separate colonial and state acts from 1680 to 1849 making slave insurrection or inciting to insurrection a criminal offense, and fixing punishments (usually capital).[44] A series of seventeen laws from 1680 to 1851 defined and prohibited "unlawful assembly" of slaves. These acts usually defined unlawful assembly as consisting of more than three or four slaves, belonging to different masters, or meeting after dark. Religious services held at night were declared unlawful assemblies by some of the acts. Other laws made conspiracy to rebel a crime, prohibited slaves or Negroes in general from carrying firearms, and made illegal the handling of medicine or drugs by slaves. Acts of a similar nature not included in these classifications included prohibition upon a free Negro entertaining a slave, requirement of one overseer for ten slaves or more, and a requirement that at least one White person be on every plantation at all times.

A slightly different type of legislation in the slave codes was directed against the possibility of slaves assimilating ideas and sentiments which were legitimate for the dominant caste. Thus, four states passed laws against allowing slaves to preach. The basis for this prohibition seems to have been a fear that slave preachers would misuse their privilege and stir up discontent. This might be taken as tacit recognition of the possibility of an inconsistency between Christianity and slavery, a point previously discussed. Seven Southern states prohibited the teaching of slaves to read and write, and two of these states had earlier colonial laws of the same sort. The largest number of laws restricting the possibility of ideas and sentiments incompatible with slavery reaching the slaves are those sometimes known as anti-abolitionist laws. These laws made it a criminal offense to publish, write, or say anything advising slaves to rebel or inimical to slavery. Although these acts, and those prohibiting education of the slaves, may have been directed against the antislavery propaganda, they were by no means directed exclusively against the "abolition" movement proper (dating from 1831) since twelve of the twenty-six laws antedated that time. Moreover, there appears to be no basis for saying that the severe features of the slave codes were due to the abolitionist propaganda, for only twenty-four of the total of sixty-four acts of the various types summarized here were passed in 1831 or later.

It has often been claimed that the laws here summarized were in fact for the most part dead letters, and only enacted by legislatures following some conspiracies, or rumors of conspiracies, some recent murder of a master by his slave, or some particularly vitriolic attack by the abolitionists. This claim undoubtedly contains a good deal of truth. But as Dumond has written,

> Grant that there was a vast difference between the theory and the practical application of the slave codes; grant, also, that the danger of general insurrection was, and was known to be, remote; and the fact remains that the slaveholders were afraid of a rational discussion of the merits of slavery.[45]

Moreover, whether the laws were strictly enforced or not, the circumstances which gave rise to them reveal an imperfect institutionalization of the slavery system. Even if some were based only on fears of revolts or escape by the slaves, they yet reveal uncertainties upon the part of the politically dominant group in regard to the stability and orderliness of the master-slave relationship.

A final indication of the fairly large departure from the idealized contentment and docility of the slave is the behavior of the Negro, both slave and free, in the Civil War. Although it is commonly supposed that the Negro slaves almost uniformly carried on plantation labor without direction from the able-bodied White males, the truth falls considerably short of that notion. Not only were patrol duties of the Whites maintained, and in some cases increased, but many slaves managed to give assistance to the invading armies.[46]

If the slave often did not quietly accept his subordinate position, to what sources may this discontent be traced? One possibility is that of the anti-slavery propaganda. This source of discontent, it has been noted, cannot be given exclusive "credit," since escapes, plots, revolts, and severe restrictions in the slave codes occurred early and late in the slavery period. Another possible source of discontent which has been previously suggested was the presence of free Negroes in the population. This danger to the stability of the slavery system might arise from the active interference of free Negroes, a danger often recognized and usually exaggerated in the laws placing restrictions upon manumission, and upon previously manumitted free Negroes. Although the free Negroes were still members of a subordinate caste, they were nominally free, and recognized as legal and social persons.

Perhaps more important than either of these sources of discontent was the adoption by the slaves of at least part of the value system of the dominant caste. Now there would be little reason to attach importance to the fact that slaves had the opportunity, or rather the necessity, of recognizing that aspirations, value-attitudes, or culture goals held as legitimate for the dominant caste were not uniformly available for the slaves, had the value system been a logically closed one. That is, if the culture goals and the institutional order had been established uniformly on a caste basis, so that those goals and value-attitudes which were legitimate for the dominant caste had no implications concerning their legitimacy for the subordinate caste, the acceptance of that value system could not be expected to lead to discontent and resistance upon the part of the lower group, but rather to stability of the system.

In the South, however, the institutional order, far from being clear and uniform, was in fact characterized by rather deep-seated uncertainties and ambivalences. In legal conception as in less formal institutional values and attitudes there was no certainty concerning the problem of the slave as an economic unit or as a social person. Although the slave was also a member of a subordinate caste, and the Negro was presumed to be a slave until he could prove his freedom, the awarding of freedom to slaves because of "meritorious services" and personal attachments (valuation of the individual slave as a person) implied liberty and evaluation as a person as legitimate goals toward which the slave might aspire. Failing any automatic, institutionally established means for achieving the goal, the slave might resort to revolt or escape. Despite the greater expectation of assimilation of dominant caste ideology on the part of the upper class of the slaves (house servants and artisans) there is some evidence that their higher status and personal recognition became qualified achievements of the goals of greater freedom and recognition, and that the discontent arose chiefly from among those slaves who were treated as economic units.

The dissatisfactions with the slavery system upon the part of the slaves appear then to have arisen from the acceptance of social values, the legitimacy of which was not uniformly and consistently denied to them either by the institutional order which provided the framework of the slavery system or by the actual developments of the master-slave relationship, and yet which were at least partially inconsistent with slavery.

AMBIGUOUS POSITION OF POOR WHITES

The slaves and free Negroes, below the caste line, were not the only groups in the population which occupied an inferior position because of the peculiar orientation of social stratification about the slavery system. The relationship of non-slaveholders, often erroneously lumped together as "poor whites," to the slavery system is also of importance in any adequate appraisal of the social order, and its elements of stability and instability. In an earlier portion of this chapter it was pointed out that a majority of the dominant caste did not own slaves. Many of these non-slaveholders belonged to the lower middle class, and only those at the bottom of the scale of stratification (that is, above the caste line), could be called "poor whites." Yet many of the others, although not strictly "poor whites," suffered both economically and socially from their subordinate position.

The key to the understanding of the support of the slavery system by non-slaveholders, particularly the poor Whites for whom there was little honorable employment, is to be found in the caste structure associated with slavery. So long as the Negro remained a slave, the poor White by definition remained superior, even though his economic position was no better or manifestly inferior. Non-slaveholders of all classes were continually held in line by the politically dominant class by emphasis upon caste rather than class. By the existence of a subordinate and servile caste all Whites became members of the dominant class. A further consideration was, however, involved in the support of slavery within the caste structure. The Negro, belonging to an inferior caste, and as a slave, did not compete so much in the *immediate* sense with White labor. The free Negro, although still a member of an inferior caste, was necessarily in a situation of competition with the poorer Whites. It is typical of caste organization that the occupation of the lower or lowest caste becomes stigmatized, and is considered degrading employment for members of a higher caste. This is one clear basis for the opposition of laboring Whites to the freeing of slaves from rough agricultural labor. White artisans were continually protesting against the intrusion of free Negroes (against whom they were moderately successful) and slaves into skilled labor.

Slavery was interpreted by the non-slaveholding Whites as essential for maintaining their superiority over the Negro, both in the occupational world and in the broader scheme of stratification. Even the limited occupational sphere allowed the Negroes, however, largely closed those types of employment to the Whites because of the association between occupation and caste. The unskilled laborer, the true "poor white," had no place open to him. Slavery and the caste system gave him a social position above that of the Negro, but took away any means of economic advancement. This set of considerations exhibits further the differential immigration into the North and South during the slavery period.

The lack of immigration to the South has been given several explanations, but chiefly that the odium attached to labor because of the slavery system made the region unattractive to immigrants. Now this interpretation is not precisely correct. It is not true that labor, even manual labor, was uniformly regarded as degrading in the South. There was, it has been observed, during the slavery regime a large, and respectable, "middle class" of yeoman farmers and independent artisans. Not all labor was despised, *per se,* but certain types of labor, typically field work and personal service were regarded as "niggers' work." White labor was set apart by economic, caste, and often geographical lines. The significant point is that the *type of labor, or the economic status,* typical of immigrants was already filled by slaves in the South. There was thus both a numerical-economic and an institutional basis for the lack of attractiveness of this labor market for the immigrant. It was not that the immigrant had to labor that reflected on his status, but that his low economic position and the effective labor demand put him in competition with slave labor. It is the failure to recognize this distinction which leads Phillips into a half-truth when he writes:

The continued avoidance of the South by the great mass of incoming Europeans in post-bellum decades has now made it clear that it was the Negro character of the slaves rather than the slave status of the Negroes which was chiefly responsible.[47]

If the foregoing analysis be substantially correct, there is no reason to hypothecate any "racial antipathy" *per se* in explanation of differential migration, for the caste criterion of division of labor, established under slavery, persisted under "freedom." What was important was neither that work was dishonorable, nor that the type of work available to immigrants was typically performed by Negroes, but that this available work was done by Negroes who as freemen or as slaves belonged to an inferior caste.

THE DEFENSE OF SLAVERY

One final range of problems remains to be examined in the analysis of the convergence of the "moral order" and the factual organization in slavery: the ideas, sentiments, and general value-attitudes maintained by pro-slavery writers.

From very early in the slavery period there had been some argument over the justification of slavery. The lead was usually taken by those opposed to slavery, and the arguments in answer to the attack were chiefly that slavery was a necessary evil as an economic system, or as a system of social control. During and immediately after the Revolutionary period, at the time that slavery was abolished in the North and at a low ebb in the South, many Southern leaders confidently expected to see slavery gradually die out. Temporary expediency was therefore the chief argument against immediate abolition. It was not until the slavery system was given a new lease on life economically and the severe abolitionist attacks had begun that the justification of slavery as a positive good became prominent.

The problem of institutional limitations upon general and diffuse culture goals is revealed in the pro-slavery literature. The defense of slavery in terms of unfortunate necessity amounted to an hierarchization of the normative elements involved. That is, there was no denial of the cogency of the appeals of the Christian ethic and the Revolutionary philosophy emphasizing the value of the individual, but the maintenance of slavery was held necessary as a means to one or more social values even more ultimate than that of the diffuse sentiment concerning the value of the individual: racial control, general social stability, or economic prosperity.

The expression of the ethical valuation of the individual, and the claim that slavery did not in fact deny its importance or its achievement arose in a variety of justifications for slavery. This attempt to rationalize the slavery system with the valuation of the individual is clear-cut in the entire gamut of sources appealing to the ideal of a mild and familistic master-slave relationship. The cruelties and deprivations to which the slaves were subject, according to anti-slavery writers, were vehemently denied.[48] The claim was made that the slaves were not only economically well provided for, but that personal master-slave relations were well established. Moreover, an attempt was made to refute charges that the sentiments of the individual slave, particularly in reference to family relationships, were disregarded, and that his moral and spiritual welfare was neglected.

Likewise showing an adherence to the value of the individual and the attempt to make slavery consistent with it were those theories denying any absolute control or ownership by the master of the body and soul of the slave. According to these theories the property of the master lay only in the labor of the slave, and not in his person. The relationship, then, it was argued, was a quasi-contractual one.

In many respects a very different type of pro-slavery thought was that seeking to establish slaves (and Negroes in general) as a special and inferior social category, to whom no values held as legitimate for the dominant caste were relevant. The racial inferiority of the Negro, it has been seen, was a well-established legal doctrine fairly early in the slavery system. Although the pro-slavery literature is permeated with this general idea, it was fairly late in the slavery period that the full "scientific" justification and ethical implications were developed. These theories took a variety of forms, but were chiefly based upon theories in physical anthropology and human morphology. Perhaps the leading argument developed was that of the "pluralists" in regard to racial origin. According to this theory, developed most fully by Dr. Josiah Clark Nott, a physician of Mobile, Alabama, the Negroes were not only inferior to the Whites, but an entirely different species which had developed independently of the White race.[49] This thesis was "demonstrated" by differences in morphological structure, skin pigmentation, and other biological aspects. The theory had many followers, and became the starting-point for further developments justifying the caste system. If the Negro were a separate and inferior species, essentially subhuman, then no foolish worries about ethical questions of the valuation of the person were necessary. He was placed in a category to which no social values or ordinary rules need apply.

Moreover, various ethnological theories gave further sanction to the caste structure. Black skin was claimed to be associated with the Negroes' racial inferiority, and not due to any climatic factors. It was even claimed that in addition to the skin, the membranes, tendons, and the "fluids" of the Negro were black, and even the brain and nerves were of a dark shade.[50] Such a theory of course was useful in fixing the black skin as an unerasable mark of inferiority. Similar support was given to the caste ideology by the presumed "hybrid weakness" of the mulatto. Racial amalgamation was therefore unthinkable.

The anthropological theories "establishing" Negro inferiority and thereby justifying slavery were in many respects simply a logical conclusion to the general assumption of inferiority, and the tendency to institutionalize slavery on that basis. At no time was the general value-attitude concerning individual worth denied, but only that all such values were relevant only to the dominant caste.

A particular application of the justification of slavery through categorization of the slave and maintaining that the value of the individual was a caste-oriented one was the development of the governmental theory of the "Greek democracy." Slavery (of the inferior) not only was held not to be antithetical to the valuation of the individual, but rather contributed to the maintenance and support of that value for those to whom it legitimately applied. Slavery was claimed to be necessary for a truly democratic or republican government by citizens. Leisure was permitted the slaveholder to develop his highest capabilities through being freed from menial tasks, adequately performed by those who had no capabilities to develop.

A final type of solution of the relation between slavery and the diffuse culture goal attaching value to the individual was one not fully worked out. It consisted in a denial, or partial denial, of the legitimacy of the culture goal. This rejection was rarely, if ever, complete, but rather took the form of denying particular forms and verbalizations of the value. Chief among these solutions was that of denying the validity of the "natural rights" doctrine and the expressions of the Declaration of Independence. Chancellor Harper, for example, denied the existence of any "natural rights," claiming all rights were established by civil society. The rights of individuals, and the development of their capabilities were claimed to be a privilege which was not universally applicable.[51] These arguments tend to merge into that of categorization, however, since the application of the value to the dominant caste is not denied.

Other pro-slavery arguments were less immediately formulable in terms of the classification here adopted, chiefly the scriptural arguments and the arguments from history and natural law. For the most part these theories neither confirmed nor denied the ethical valuation of the individual, and therefore did not discuss its relation to the slavery system. Their orientation was primarily forensic: anti-slavery attacks were answered by appeals to authority.

This summary of the pro-slavery arguments, brief and perhaps inadequate, nevertheless suggests the orientation of the Southern social situation on the ideological level to the general value-attitude attaching worth to the individual, and the necessity felt on that level to find some basis for justifying an officially established and institutionally supported slavery system which had been publicly called to attention as antithetical to that value-attitude. The justifications of the slavery system that have been noted were no more uniform than the institutional patterns of that system. If the analysis of the elements involved in the situation be substantially correct as here presented, the concrete master-slave relationship, the institutional order, and, finally, the ideological arguments demonstrate not only an acceptance of the general and diffuse culture goal, but also the relevance of that culture goal at various crucial places in the social structure. The relative indeterminacy of the entire social structure in its orientation to the slavery system appears therefore to be further corroboration of the basic ambivalence between conceptions of the slave as property and as a person noted in the legal status of slavery. The entire slavery system, therefore, appears to have been imperfectly integrated with a basic and important goal in the society.

VI

The Anti-Slavery Attack

Slavery was known as the "peculiar institution" of the South. In previous chapters some of the peculiarities of that "peculiar institution" have been discussed. But if slavery was peculiar to the South, the problems of slavery were not. The social order of which slavery was a part was primarily the immediate one which gave it legal sanction and economic significance. It was also, however, part of a broader social order—the nation—and whether Southern slaveholders liked it or not certain people in the North also felt it necessary to be concerned with a system with which they were not immediately involved.

EARLY CRITICISM OF SLAVERY

The opposition to slavery did not appear full-grown, without benefit of ancestry, during the later period when slavery was in fact peculiar to the South, nor was it always exclusively generated in the North. The idea of an inconsistency between the Christian ethic and slavery, particularly the enslavement of Christians, arose rather early in both sections. Active opposition to slavery before the Revolutionary period was chiefly of a religious nature, and came not so much from the Puritans of New England as from Quakers, North and South.[1]

The Puritans believed in the equality of human souls, but man, as touching nature, was but a worm of this earth; the Quakers believed in the dignity of man and in a human brotherhood which included social equality as well as equality before God and law . . . [2]

Ideologies developing prior to and during the Revolution gave impetus and direction to earlier anti-slavery sentiment. "The two movements, Revolution and anti-slavery, one tending toward the independence of the White race, and the other toward freedom of the Black, were in fact intimately connected throughout the colonial period. . . . Theological doctrines and philosophical theories contributed to both alike, and it was in the period of the American Revolution that the slender streams of anti-slavery sentiment, which had been flowing in separate channels for nearly a century, united and gathered force for efficient action." [3]

During the Revolutionary period and in the years immediately following, abolition societies were organized in both the North and South. Abolition was accomplished in the North, but by 1803 the number of anti-slavery societies in the South was very small.[4] Following the prohibition of the African slave-trade in 1808 the amount of anti-slavery activity lagged for a number of years, but by no means completely died out. The American Colonization Society, an organization attempting to provide means of returning Negroes to an African colony—Liberia—was no more than mildly anti-slavery, and often not that. In the South it was supported chiefly in the hope of getting rid of free Negroes. There were 251 local organizations between 1819 and 1832, 105 in the North and

146 in the South. All but 36 of the Southern organizations, however, were in the "border states" of Delaware, Virginia, Maryland, Kentucky, Tennessee, and the District of Columbia.[5]

A large number of anti-slavery societies were organized between 1808 and 1831, chiefly through the efforts of Benjamin Lundy.[6] Although he worked in both the North and the South, his success in the latter section was chiefly confined to the border states.

All the [anti-slavery] societies that have been mentioned [in the South] were in the border states or those Southern states immediately bordering on them, and it is most probable that there were few or none in the true South, with the exception of North Carolina. This point should be borne in mind when the comparison between North and South in regard to the number of societies is made.[7]

Lundy started publication of *The Genius of Universal Emancipation* at Mount Pleasant, Ohio, in 1821, and later that year published it at Jonesborough, Tennessee, where he continued until 1824. In 1824 he began publication at Baltimore. In the course of his numerous organizing expeditions he met William Lloyd Garrison in Boston in 1828. Garrison joined him in Baltimore in 1829 to assist in editing the paper. Garrison was more outspoken, was put in jail, fined, and left town. Garrison did not again get south of the Mason and Dixon line, but he made himself known in those parts.

ABOLITIONISTS BECOME MILITANT

In January, 1831, Garrison published the first issue of a militant abolitionist newspaper, *The Liberator*. The direction and intensity of attacks upon slavery were set in that issue. He wrote:

I am aware that many object to the severity of my language; but is there not cause for severity? I *will* be as harsh as truth, and as uncompromising as justice. On this subject, I do not wish to think, or speak, or write, with moderation . . . urge me not to use moderation in a cause like the present. I am in earnest—I will not equivocate—I will not excuse—I will not retreat a single inch— AND I WILL BE HEARD.[8]

Until 1840 the "New Abolitionists" under the leadership of Garrison were a militant minority group in New England. Other groups in the Middle Atlantic states and in the West were also active, although not under Garrison's leadership. The press was the chief propaganda instrument of these groups, and in the middle '30's the volume of literature distributed had reached rather large proportions. In the peak year of 1835 the following figures were reported to the American Anti-Slavery Society.

	For Year
Human Rights, about 20,000 per month	240,000
Anti-Slavery Record, 25,000 per month	385,000
Emancipator, 15,000 per month	210,000
Slave's Friend, 15,000 per month	205,000
Quarterly Anti-Slavery	5,500
Life of Greenville Sharpe	2,000
Bound Volumes	1,000
Mrs. Child's Appeal	1,000
Slave's Friend (bound volume)	5,000
Occasional Pamphlets	8,500
Circulars	36,000

Abolition was by no means a mass movement in the North. The militant abolitionists remained a minority, and often not a welcome one. Nor did the anti-slavery movement escape the fate of many minority movements: internal dissension. Garrison and his immediate followers were uncompromising extremists. Political action they viewed as compromise. Since slavery was tacitly recognized by the Constitution, and Southern slaveholders held office under it, some abolitionists disavowed any allegiance to it. One of Garrison's boldest gestures was the burning of a copy of the United States Constitution at a Fourth of July celebration at Newton,

Massachusetts, in 1854. With great pomp and circumstance the Constitution was declared to be "a covenant with death and agreement with hell."[10] In 1840 the American Anti-Slavery Society convention was split over the question of—of all things—feminism. The feminist movement had the support of Garrison, and *vice versa*. Other anti-slavery leaders were less concerned with consistency and with making no compromises than they were with establishing an effective means for combatting slavery. Thus after 1840 the anti-slavery movement made most headway in political circles, and Garrison passed out of the limelight.[11] Anti-slavery argument did not.

Early and late, militant abolitionists and moderate anti-slavery workers, non-political propagandists and political orators, the mode of orientation remained essentially alike: argument and appeals to sentiment. It is with these arguments, and the sentiments or value-attitudes to which they appealed, or which they assumed, that the present analysis is chiefly concerned. To what policies, economic interests, or ethical convictions was slavery considered antithetical?

THE ARGUMENTS AGAINST SLAVERY

The earliest arguments against slavery were of a religious character. This was true until just prior to and during the Revolutionary period, when the appeals to natural and inalienable rights as applying to the Negro slave became paramount. Old Puritans like John Eliot and Cotton Mather were less concerned about slavery itself than some of the observed incidents of slavery—primarily the failure to care for the moral and religious instruction of the slave.[12] In 1700 Judge Samuel Sewall wrote his famous anti-slavery essay, "The Selling of Joseph," [13] in which he argued that slavery broke up Negro families, and was an evil not offset by any resultant good involved in the conversion of the Negro. He further argued that slavery was detrimental to the master's morality.

A number of Quakers, among whom John Woolman was the most outstanding, opposed slavery early in the eighteenth century on grounds of its denial of a human brotherhood before God. Later men like Benjamin Franklin, Thomas Jefferson, and Thomas Paine decried the demoralizing influence of slavery on both master and slave. The attacks upon slavery in the Revolutionary period largely appealed to the same sentiments as the previous ones, but added terms from the new philosophy.

During the later slavery period (1831–1860) few of the basic arguments were changed, but new variations were added, and a few defensive answers to pro-slavery thought appeared. The volume of anti-slavery literature during this period was enormous. A bibliography of several thousand items would be required to canvass the field. Investigation in connection with the present study, however, revealed that the mass of literature was characterized more by its uniformities than by its variety. Repetitious insistence played a greater part in the propaganda than novel arguments. Whereas in the earlier period each book or pamphlet attempted to establish one or two arguments, the later tendency was to assemble the combined heritage from earlier opponents of slavery and repeat until exhausted. There is accordingly no apparent reason to attempt to cite all the propaganda literature in this analysis, since added numbers would have only statistical significance.

The moral and religious arguments continued to uphold top "honors." That slavery constituted a hindrance to moral and religious instruction of the Negro was emphasized continually. Thus, Horace Mann, in a speech before the House of Representatives in 1848, declared that slavery prevented the development of conscience, or the "dearest and most precious of all human rights," the right of private judgment in matters of religion.[14] Although this general argument might imply nothing concerning the ethical valuation of the individual as a social person—not simply as a religious soul—it typically expressed or implied this conviction. The immorality of slavery in breaking up slave families—depriving slaves of ties of human affection, failure to recognize marriage and legitimize children—was a constant source of argumentative ammunition.[15] The failure of slavery to provide values and status belonging inherently to human beings was again the point of contention.

The detrimental effect of slavery upon the morality of the master was an argument little used in the later period, since the attacks upon slavery were merged with attacks upon the slaveholder, and upon the South as a whole. The presumed demoralising effect of slavery on the slaveholder was apparently now deemed unnecessary to emphasize.

The general argument against slavery on the ground of a human brotherhood before God was widely implied in other arguments, but was more or less taken for granted as needing no new emphasis.[16] Likewise, that the seeming inferiority of the Negro, and his immorality were the result of a debasement of human nature through his enslavement came to be accepted as a common assumption.[17]

The attack upon the original religious justification of slavery in terms of the heathen condition of the Negro, by claiming that there was no reason for choosing the Negro rather than any other heathen, was chiefly of historical significance, when such a justification was relied upon.[18] But the religious argument in defense of or opposition to slavery did not end there. The battle of the Scriptures raged furiously. In view of the advantage given the South by reason of the passages giving open or tacit approval to slavery,[19] the anti-slavery attack was based chiefly upon the inconsistency of the slavery system with the Golden Rule and with the general Christian ethic. A large number of the appeals to sentiment in anti-slavery literature were expressed in terms of the sinfulness of slaveholding, the sacrifice of the Christian view of the moral value and dignity of the individual, and the idea that a human soul could be owned by another human. Horace Mann, for example, considered it an outrage to morality and Christianity to consider slaves in the same class as cattle.[20] In taking this position anti-slavery writers rejected any basic dualism between "things of this world" and "things of the spirit," and assumed that acceptance of the Christian ethic implied a valuation of the social individual. The slave was thus not only claimed to have a soul, a point rarely denied, but also that this had wider implications in his valuation as a person.

A final type of moral and religious argument was in a sense a defensive one; the crime of enslavement was not justified by the presumed beneficial effect of conversion.[21] This argument again necessarily implies a rejection of a radical dualism, and insistence upon social rights of the individual slave.

A second major category of arguments against slavery, less important numerically and in point of intensity, than the moral and religious arguments, was yet in some cases closely akin to them. These comprised social and political objections to slavery. Perhaps most closely related to those previously considered was the argument that education, necessary for the development of the individual to his proper position and value, was denied to the Negro slave. This is a clear case of assuming the culture goal of the valuation of the individual, and an attack upon the failure to provide the necessary means for developing the individual to his fullest capacities. That the denial of this symbolically important mark of individual worth was official and legal only served to call it more clearly to attention. The "poor whites" were also judged to be the victims of the slavery system, not only in regard to political and economic opportunities, but also in regard to proper development through education.[22]

Other minor social and political objections to slavery were fairly numerous, but typically incidental to arguments on an ethical basis. For example, Benjamin Franklin had earlier maintained that slavery reduced the birth rate of the population in general, and this point was repeated several times.[23] Another objection to slavery was essentially an answer to the "Greek democracy" theory of slavery, namely, that freedom and liberty were tender or insecure, and could not thrive alongside slavery. This was an argument frequently raised in the debates over extension of slavery into the new territories of the West, especially in reply to the common Southern justification of expansion as an "extension of the area of freedom." Concerning this general debate Weinberg has noted:

It was . . . true that, as anti-expansionists charged, "we were to extend the area of freedom by enlarging the boundary of slavery." But it was not true that, as anti-expansionists also charged, the phrase about extending freedom was used merely to cover up the design of extending slavery. The strange truth of the matter is that the extension of slavery, which virtually no Southern expansionist denied to be one of his motives, did not seem to the slaveholder incompatible with the ideal of diffusing democracy. The harmonization of the two purposes is explained in part by the Southerner's belief that religious and natural law made the negro a necessary exception to the principle of political equality. But it is also explained by the fact that the extension of slavery appeared essential to States' liberties. In this view the Southerner overlooked the consideration that slavery seemed to abolitionist sections an equal infringement of their right to a union based on universal individual liberty.[24]

The legal and political discussion of slavery had many ramifications. The whole legal sanction of slavery was denounced on the ground that there could be no property right in stolen goods, and never a property right in another man for whatever reason. A Massachusetts court, for example, held that slavery is a relation founded in force, not in right, existing, where it does exist, by force of positive law, and not recognized as founded in natural right, as intimated by the definition of slavery in the civil law. . . .[25]

Somewhat related was the question of the relation of slavery to the Constitution. The opinions of anti-slavery writers on this question were not expressed in terms of opposition to slavery, which was assumed, but whether the Constitution was intended to support slavery, and if so, if abolitionists owed it any allegiance. As previously noted, the Garrisonian abolitionists branded the Constitution as a slaveholders' document and preached disunion under the slogan: "No Union with Slaveholders." [26] On the other hand, there were those who insisted that it was the intention of the framers of the Constitution to limit the extension of slavery, and that they had in mind its early disappearance.

The problem of the feasibility of emancipation and its desirability for civil order gained some attention. In answer to Southern arguments that emancipation of the slaves was impossible because of the disorder which would follow, the anti-slavery writers maintained that emancipation was an absolutely safe public policy.[27] In fact, the charge was levelled in the opposite direction: that slavery was dangerous to civil order, in view of possible servile insurrections.[28]

Arguments against slavery as an economic system were by no means wanting. From early general declarations that abolition was an economic necessity,[29] the claims became more specific. For example, it was maintained that slave labor was more expensive than free labor, and that slavery was the cause of the lack of industrial development in the South.[30] Other arguments were pertinent to slavery as an economic system, but the animus of attack was the failure of that economic system to conform to ideals held by anti-slavery writers. The presumed stigma which slavery placed upon labor raised the issue of the dignity of labor, and the feeling that the laborer should be "worthy of his hire." This touched strongly upon the Puritanic ideal of hard and honest labor as a Christian duty, and the development of talents and acquisition of the fruits of labor as an index of God's favor.[31] The failure of the labor system of the South to provide honorable employment for the "poor whites" was another point of attack, and this was coupled with the objections to the economic and political oligarchy of slaveholders in the South.[32]

A large quantity of anti-slavery propaganda may be called primarily sentimental or emotional. As Turner correctly observes:

Opposition to slavery on purely sentimental grounds was not, in the strict sense of the term, argument, for it was generally devoid of the intellectual element; yet, what it lacked in this respect, it more than supplied in the strong emotional appeal, and thus became an effective means of promoting the anti-slavery cause.[33]

The moral, religious, social, and economic movement against slavery during this period was sufficient to convince thousands of Northern people, hitherto hostile or indifferent to abolition, of the injustice of slavery. But something more was needed than mere conviction of its injustice. The people had to be moved to action. The sentimental arguments attempted to accomplish this result.[34]

The sentimental or emotional propaganda was largely argument by example: the cruelty and injustice of slavery. A few examples of this literature will suffice to illustrate the type.

"Dr. K., a man of wealth and a practising physician in the county of Yazoo, state of Mississippi, personally known to me, having lived in the same neighborhood more than twelve months, after having scourged one of his negroes for running away, declared with an oath, that if he ran away again, he would kill him. The negro, as soon as an opportunity offered ran away again. He was caught and brought back. Again he was scourged, until his flesh, mangled and torn, and thick mingled with the clotted blood, rolled from his back. He became apparently insensible, and beneath the heaviest stroke would scarcely utter a groan. The master got tired, laid down his whip and nailed the Negro's ear to a tree; in this condition, nailed fast to the rugged wood, he remained all night!

"Suffice it to say, in the conclusion, that the next day he was found DEAD." [35]

"A negro was tied up, and flogged until the blood ran down and filled his shoes, so that when he raised either foot and set it down again, the blood would run over their tops. I could not look on any longer, but turned away in horror; the whipping was continued to the number of 300 lashes as I understand; a quart of spirits of terpentine was then applied to his lacerated body. . . . The crime for which the negro was whipped, was that of telling the other negroes, that *the overseer had lain with his wife.*" [36]

Although not argumentative, the citing of cruel and unjust treatment of the slave nevertheless assumed an ethical conviction that the actions recounted were really cruel and unjustified. This necessarily involved a denial of the propriety of the complete domination of the master over the slave, and a feeling that such treatment of a fellow human being was unsupportable. Certainly sentiments concerning the dignity of the person, integrity of the individual, and the like were taken for granted in this propaganda, else it would have had little meaning. "Cruelty," even of the extreme type painted by the anti-slavery writers, always rests upon a value judgment, however amorphous, concerning the proper limits of extension of physical coercion.

One very interesting example cited against slavery did not involve actual physical cruelty, but clearly fits into the sentiments in regard to integrity of the body. Weld quotes and comments on a "late Prospectus of the South Carolina Medical College . . ." which contains the following passage:

"Some advantages of a peculiar character are connected with this institution, which it may be proper to point out. No place in the United States offers as great opportunities for the acquisition of anatomical knowledge, subjects being obtained from among the colored population in sufficient number for every purpose, and proper dissections carried on without offending any individuals in the community."

Without offending any individuals in the community! More than half the population of Charleston, we believe, is 'colored;' their graves may be ravaged, their dead may be dug up, dragged into the dissecting room, exposed to the gaze, heartless gibes, and experimenting knives, of a crowd of inexperienced operators, who are given to understand in the prospectus, that, if they do not acquire manual dexterity in dissection, it will be wholly their own fault, in neglecting to improve the unrivalled advantages afforded by the institution—since each can have as many human bodies as he pleases to experiment upon—and as to the fathers, mothers, husbands, wives, brothers, and sisters, of those whom they cut to pieces from day to day, why, they are not 'individuals in the community,' but 'property.' . . .[37]

An especially large number of arguments not included in the foregoing types may, for want of a better term, be called the philosophical. That is, they made direct and express appeal to the doctrines of natural and inalienable rights, and insisted upon the applicability of these tenets to the Negro slaves. These arguments stem chiefly from the Revolutionary period,[38] but continued in full force thereafter. A group of abolitionists of Massachusetts in 1836 declared concerning inalienable rights:

This doctrine comprises an essential part of our religion—the whole of our republicanism—the whole of our abolitionism. These terms, in our vocabulary, are synonymous and indivisible.[39]

Although anti-slavery writers were primarily concerned with the slavery system, the doctrine of racial inferiority was also denied, and some attention was paid to the free Negroes, both in the North and in the South. When these questions were noted at all, the arguments against slavery were held to apply to the caste system.[40] Although there was a good deal of truth in the charge of pro-slavery writers that the abolitionists were "picking the mote from their brother's eye, while neglecting the beam in their own," these writers consistently failed to see that the basis for this almost exclusive interest in slavery, rather than in the condition of free Negroes or of Northern laborers, "wage slavery," was an *official and established* denial of the value-attitudes of the abolitionists, while Northern workers and free Negroes were nominally free and possession of their "natural rights," personal worth and dignity, and so on.

A schematic summary of the arguments against slavery, together with an indication of their relation, or lack of relation to the general ethical valuation of the individual may serve to point up the significance of that conviction in the opposition to the slavery system.[41]

I. MORAL AND RELIGIOUS
   1. Slavery is a hindrance to the moral and religious instruction of the Negro.
   2. Slavery breaks up Negro families, and thus destroys important emotional ties.

3. Slavery is detrimental to the master's morality.
4. There is a human brotherhood before God.
5. The apparent inferiority and immorality of the Negro is a result of the debasement of human nature through slavery.
6. There is no inherent reason for selecting the Negro, rather than any any other pagan, for slavery.
7. Slavery is not warranted on Scriptural grounds, and is in positive contradiction to the general principles of Christianity.
8. The crime of enslavement is not justified by the presumed beneficial effect of conversion.

II. Social and Political

1. Education, necessary for development of the individual to his proper worth, is denied the slave.
2. Slavery deprives poor Whites of proper social (including educational and political) opportunities.
3. Slavery reduces the birth rate of the whole population.
4. Freedom is tender (or insecure) and cannot thrive alongside slavery.
5. There can be no property right in stolen goods, or in another man for whatever reason.
6. The Constitution approves slavery and is not to be supported.
7. It was the intention of the framers of the Constitution to limit the extension of slavery, and they thought it would soon disappear.
8. Emancipation is safe.
9. Slavery is dangerous to the civil order.

III. Economic

1. Abolition is an economic necessity.
2. Free labor is less expensive than slave labor.
3. Industry does not flourish in the slave states.
4. Slavery, through attaching a stigma to work, reduces the willingness of the Whites to work.
5. Slavery deprives poor Whites of any honorable employment.
6. Slavery leads to concentration of wealth and political power.

IV. Sentimental and Emotional
   1. Slavery is cruel.
   2. Slavery is unjust.

V. Philosophical
   1. Natural and inalienable rights apply to the Negro, but are denied to him by slavery.

VI. Racial
   1. Negroes are not racially inferior, and the arguments against slavery apply also to the disabilities placed on free Negroes.

This summary re-emphasizes the pronounced importance in anti-slavery doctrines or arguments and appeals implying or assuming a general ethical valuation of the individual. Modes of expression, specific questions and debates, and the emotionality of the arguments all varied widely. But the arguments most strongly emphasized and most often repeated were appeals to a general sentiment that the individual person had some moral or ethical worth, and that slavery denied to the slave the availability or recognition of the legitimacy of this diffuse culture goal.

The Intersection of Reform Movements

The importance of such a value-attitude in the abolitionist campaign seems to be further corroborated by the relations of the movement to other reform movements of the period. During the 1830's and the two subsequent decades reform was in the air, particularly in the Northeast. The feminist movement was clearly allied with that of the abolitionists. Women's anti-slavery societies were organized, and one of the chief causes for the split in the ranks of the abolitionists in 1840, previously noted, was the insistence of Garrison and his immediate followers that the doctrines maintained in opposition to slavery applied also to women.[42] The "Female Anti-Slavery Societies" combined abolitionism and feminism. One correspondent wrote to a national convention: "arduous and responsible labor is before you—the iron shackle that drags heavily along the plains of the South, and the golden fetter hugged by so many of our sex, are alike to be broken!" [43]

This was also the period of a well-developed temperance movement, the rapid growth of, and interest in, popular education, and the beginnings of an effective labor movement. This seemed truly to be the period marked by the "Rise of the Common Man." [44] Moreover, those primarily interested in one type of reform were often actively engaged in one or more of the other movements. A similar overlapping in England during this same period has been emphasized by Klingberg.

Reformers did not devote themselves solely to one cause. The man who was interested in the destruction of the slave trade was generally interested also in better government for India, or in the founding of missionary societies, in teaching the people of England their letters or in prison reform, in wiser poor relief or in hospitals for the sick. [45]

Of particular importance in relating the anti-slavery movement to the social situation in the North is the recognition of the problems arising from industrialization and the growth of a propertyless laboring class. For the anti-slavery movement was primarily, almost exclusively, a lower-class movement. Abolitionists, with very few exceptions, were not drawn from among industrial and commercial leaders, nor for a long time from among the politically powerful, but from at most the lower middle classes. Their earliest and most violent opposition came from the upper classes in their own communities. Presses were wrecked, leaders mobbed and driven out, not by bands of "lawless ruffians," but by "respectable members of the community." Garrison's press in Boston was wrecked, and his life endangered by a mob composed chiefly of State Street brokers and "young men about town." This was typical of a large number of incidents in the propaganda activities of the abolitionists. [46] Angelina Grimke wrote in 1836 that, "The

Ladies' Anti-Slavery Society of Boston was called last fall, to a severe trial of their faith and constancy. They were mobbed by 'the gentlemen of property and standing' in that city at their anniversary meeting. . . ." [47] She further maintained that Northern statesmen were equally guilty with the Southern. "The interests of the North, you must know, my friends, are very closely combined with the South." [48]

It was perhaps true, as pro-slavery writers delighted in pointing out, that the "wage-slavery" of the North left little to be preferred economically to the slavery of the Negro in the South. The factory operatives of England and New England were compared with the slaves of the South, and the advantage was claimed to lie with the latter.[49] Orestes Brownson, a champion of the Northern working class, insisted that the movement against Negro slavery was in compensation for the poor working conditions of the North. Horace Greeley, liberal editor, refused to participate fully in the anti-slavery campaign.

You will readily understand that, if I regard your enterprize with less absorbing interest than you do, it is not that I deem Slavery a less but a greater evil. If I am less troubled concerning the Slavery prevalent in Charleston and New-Orleans, it is because I see so much Slavery in New York, which appears to claim my first efforts. . . . [I would not] undertake to say that the Slavery of the South is not more hideous in kind and degree than that which prevails at the North. The fact that it is more flagrant and palpable renders opposition to it comparatively easy and its speedy downfall certain. But how can I devote myself to a crusade against distant servitude, when I discern its essence pervading my immediate community and neighborhood?

I understand by Slavery, that condition in which one human being exists mainly as a convenience for other human beings—in which the time, the exertions, the faculties of a part of the Human Family are made to subserve, not their own development, physical, intellectual, and moral, but the comfort, advantage, or caprices of others. . . . In short, wherever service is rendered from one human being to another . . . where the relation . . . is one not of affection and reciprocal good offices, but of authority, social ascendency and power over subsistence on the one hand, and of necessity, servility, and degradation on the other—there, in my view, is Slavery.[50]

Greeley's view was not, however, the general one. A comparison between the economic status of Negro slaves and of Northern workers was not the only significant comparison to be made. The symbolic importance of slavery was great. It was interpreted as a definite and official denial of or infringement upon a general sentiment which permeated the reform movements: the dignity and worth of the individual. It might be true that "the abolitionists never had time to investigate the nature of slavery. He was too busy denouncing it. He could deduce its practice from its nature. He could also estimate the character and quality of those who were depraved enough to hold slaves. Little else in the region interested him. So gradually, anything peculiar to the section, especially if it were bad, was ascribed to the influence of slavery. . . ."[51] It did not follow, from the fact that "Perhaps the idea of slavery was always worse than the fact itself,"[52] that only the "facts" were important and the idea was not. Perusal of the anti-slavery literature confirms the view that the mere admission on the part of the Southerners that slavery existed was felt to be an indication of moral turpitude, and that to defend slavery was adding insult to injury. To fail to recognize the inconsistency felt by those opposed to slavery to exist between a variety of sentiments, centering about the value of the individual, and the slavery system is to be led astray by claiming that there were no important values at stake, that those opposed to slavery were completely insincere, and so on. To place exclusive emphasis upon the economic condition in the Northeast, or the failure of anti-slavery workers to campaign effectively in behalf of Northern free Negroes is to fail utterly to comprehend the intensity of the moral opposition to slavery.

The slavery system ran into difficulties in the section in which it was a "peculiar institution" because of the difficulty on both the institutional and the action levels of establishing its relationship to a diffuse, but nonetheless real value-attitude concerning the ethical valuation of the individual. This difficulty was blatantly and persistently pointed out by those outside the immediate system, who fairly uniformly maintained or assumed the relevance of this value-attitude to the slavery system. The specific motivations of the attackers may have been, in fact probably were, various, but their insistence upon the ethical valuation of the individual lends further corroboration not only of the general importance of this culture goal, but also of its concrete relevance to the slavery system. Divergent sectional interests and different economies were certainly at stake in the controversy. So were the relations between the institutions of slavery and ideas concerning the worth of the individual.

VII

Retrospect

The slavery system may be said to be basically a mode of labor management and economic organization. For this point of view there is both historical and analytical support. In the concrete development of the slavery system the question of labor utilization was found to be paramount. In the situation of free, or nearly free, land in the early American colonies wage labor was impossible, since laborers preferred self-sufficiency on the land to economic dependence upon others. White indentured servitude was the first solution found for the labor problem, and under the semi-commercial economy, particularly of the South, a continuous supply of labor was important. The introduction of Negroes had at first no further significance than that of adding to the available labor supply, under a fictitious extension of the indenture contract. Although the transition to a slavery system was of wider significance, and was clearly dependent upon drawing lines of differentiation between White and Negro laborers, its immediate import was that of "relationships of production." In Chapter I the early development of the slavery system was analyzed, particularly in reference to the comparative importance of slavery in the economies of the Northern and Southern colonies. The commercial agriculture of the South was found to be more dependent upon a large labor supply than was the small-farm and trading economy of the North. Slavery was introduced into both sections, but its role in the South was much larger than in the North. Although throughout the period from 1650 to 1770 there was evidence of uncertainty about the ethical justification of slavery, this became crucial roughly during the Revolutionary period. It was at this time that emancipation of slaves was accomplished or set in motion in the Northern states and seriously questioned in the South.

This comparative analysis established the importance of the ethical opposition to slavery, but also the relevance of differential economic conditions to the divergent results. From this time wage labor became the labor system of the North, subsequently in an industrial economy, and slavery the "peculiar institution" of the South. A brief discussion of the Northern labor system, in Chapter II, pointed to the development of a labor demand, filled through pre-paid immigration, *after* the slavery system had been abolished.

In the "mature" slavery system the economic organization was again in a certain sense basic. Slavery was tied into, and to a large extent dependent upon, a commercial agricultural economy. In Chapter III the economics of slavery was discussed in some detail, particularly in relation to the plantation type of agriculture. The problems of "soil exhaustion" and expansion were found to have been chiefly significant in relation to a competitive market economy and an inadequate labor supply. The doctrine of the unprofitableness of slavery as a mode of labor organization was examined and found wanting. In fact the great profitableness of slavery in the plantation system in the newer regions of the Southwest, where the polar type of the purely economic nexus of relationship was approached, was the source of some of the economic difficulties in the older regions. But that the slavery-plantation organization was profitable in individual cases does not mean that it was satisfactory for the region as a whole. The majority of Whites were non-slaveholders, and for the lower classes of these, the slavery and caste systems, which made the types of manual labor performed by slaves dishonorable, militated against their economic well-being. The slavery system thus failed to utilize not only the full productive capacity of the slave, but of the poorer White people as well. The source of this situation was not to be found in the economics of slavery, but in the legal and institutional definitions of social status.

Slavery was accordingly much more than an economic system. Economic relationships took place within a wider institutional framework. The early establishment of slavery was not an automatic process, but depended upon some sort of formulation of who might be slaves, and of what constituted slavery. In the discussion of the legal status of slavery in Chapter IV it appeared that these problems, and others related to them, were solved only slowly, and never completely. The justification of slavery upon grounds of the heathen condition of the Negro raised the question of the status of the converted slave. The incompatibility felt to exist between the master-slave relationship and that of Christian persons was clear-cut and not easily dismissed. Even the subsequent racial justification, whereby slavery became the presumptive status of Negroes, and the criterion of visibility became formalized, was found to entail serious problems in respect to the free Negro and the children resulting from interracial miscegenation. The examination of the legal status of slavery demonstrated that on this level—the formal one—at least, slavery was not at all a determinate system. It was observed, moreover, that, early and late, the principal aspect of this indeterminacy was that involved in an ambivalent conception of the status of the Negro slave: was he a person or a piece of property? In short, the difficulties arising in the law of slavery point to the acceptance of an ethical valuation of the individual, and the relevance of this general value-attitude to the legal definition and justification of slavery.

The institutional rules giving sanction to the slavery system were also found to be indeterminate. The actual variation between polar extremes of a familistic feudalism on the one hand and a sheerly exploitative management on the other was reflected on the institutional level. The treatment of a slave as a piece of property, or as a representative of an inferior social category, might obviate the necessity on the social relationship level of considering the slave as a person. Any ethical convictions regarding the dignity of the person or the fulfillment of his highest capabilities might therefore be irrelevant. But this still ran counter to the idealized picture of slavery as a familistic relationship. This difficulty was found in striking form in the almost universal condemnation of the slave-trader, whose interest was admittedly a solely economic one. Yet the recognition of individual qualities and achievements, and the forming of emotional ties that admitted the relevance of the ethical valuation of the individual raised questions concerning the justice of slavery as a system placing definite limitations upon the status of the slave in the social order. Moreover, manumitting slaves for meritorious service was a tacit admission not only that slavery was not the automatic and inevitable status of Negroes— and thus contrary to the desired acceptance by the slaves of their position—but also that individual worth might be recognized and rewarded. Although, as further pointed out in Chapter V, support of the slavery system by non-slaveholding Whites was fairly effectively insured by the orientation of the class structure to the slavery regime, making slaveholding a goal for legitimate aspiration by non-slaveholders, and by the caste system which made the position of Whites superior to that of Negroes, whatever their relative economic position, the class and caste structure had elements of instability. The slaves did not uniformly accept their lot, and at least a part of the discontent was traced to an acceptance on the part of the slaves of the legitimacy for them of a culture goal of the dominant caste: freedom, and the development of the qualities and capabilities of the person. The free Negro, moreover, although officially free, was subject to caste law, and was of symbolic danger to the slavery system. Even the slaveholders, regardless of their ability to evade any inconsistency of ideas and institutions in the internal social situation, had this inconsistency persistently called to their attention by those outside the immediate social order. A large quantity of literature justifying slavery accordingly appeared, some of it perhaps representing sincere beliefs, and much of it representing rationalizations.

Finally, the slavery system was also part of a broader social system that included the North. It was subject to a continuous barrage of verbalized attacks by certain portions of the population of the North who had no immediate stake in the slavery system. From the early periods of slavery, and increasing in volume and intensity in the later period, there was an ever-larger number of Northerners who opposed slavery. An analysis of the anti-slavery arguments revealed that the largest portion of the appeals used or assumed the value-attitude of the worth of the human individual. Not only the specific features of the master-slave relationship, but the very idea of slavery, were felt to be opposed to natural and inalienable rights, dignity of the person, integrity of the individual, and similar verbalizations of the general and diffuse value-attitude. Assuming this as a legitimate culture goal, slavery was examined and found wanting, since it was felt to put unjust and improper limitations upon the achievement of that goal. This too, then, was in the broader social system an indication of the relevance of ideas to the institutions of slavery.

It is a notorious fact that in sociological analysis, as in morality and the graphic arts, it is difficult to know where to draw lines. At numerous points in the present study the possibility of further elaboration or of the examination of tangential considerations have been suggested. In addition to such studies as the comparative analysis of the various reform movements which were carried on at the same time as the abolitionist campaign, in respect to types of membership and extent of overlapping, and the arguments and appeals to sentiment employed, an extension of the analysis of the social structure of the South into the post-war period might well be undertaken. The comparative position of classes and castes in the ante-bellum and post-bellum periods, particularly in relation to the institutional reorientation necessitated by the abolition of slavery, needs further examination. The persistence of the marked economic and social disadvantages of American Negroes more than a hundred years after the official abolition of slavery indicates the continuing effects of history on the present. The change of civil status from slavery to "freedom" without according full civil rights had consequences not resolved today. The persistence of surreptitious servitude through peonage and gross economic discrimination against Negroes has only recently provoked new counterparts of the Abolition Movement. The inconsistency has once more become official, at long last. These and similar problems have necessarily been passed by in the present study. If the utilization of "historical cases" for sociological analysis has any utility at all, the historical cases are available. For the study of some of them this investigation may serve as an introduction.

Appendix

Notes to the Chapters

Chapter I

1. Lewis Cecil Gray, *History of Agriculture in the Southern United States to 1860* (Washington: Carnegie Institution, 1933), Vol. I, pp. 342–343.
2. In addition to Gray (cited in the previous note), see U. B. Phillips, *American Negro Slavery* (New York: D. Appleton and Co., 1918), Chaps. V–VI; James Curtis Ballagh "White Servitude in the Colony of Virginia," *Johns Hopkins University Studies in Historical and Political Science*, Series XIII, Nos. 6–7, June–July, 1895; Eugene Irving McCormac, "White Servitude in Maryland," in *ibid.*, Series XXII, Nos. 3–4, March–April, 1904.
3. See Phillips (cited in note 2), p. 99.
4. *Ibid.*, pp. 99–101.
5. See Carl Frederick Geiser, "Redemptioners and Indentured Servants in the Commonwealth of Pennsylvania," Supplement to *Yale Review*, 10 (2): August 1901. See also Ballagh, "White Servitude in Virginia" (cited in note 2).
6. See Ballagh (work cited in note 2), pp. 33–34.
7. See McCormac (work cited in note 2), pp. 33–36.

8. Gray (work cited in note 1), Vol. I, p. 348.
9. *Ibid.*
10. See Gray (work cited in note 1), Vol. I, pp. 351–353; Phillips (work cited in note 2), pp. 73–76.
11. See Phillips (work cited in note 2), pp. 76–77.
12. Gray (work cited in note 1), Vol. I, p. 363. The argument here is principally drawn from this source, pp. 361–371.
13. *Ibid.*, p. 371.
14. See H. A. Wyndham, *The Atlantic and Slavery* (London: Humphrey Milford, Oxford University Press, 1935), Part III.
15. See W. E. Burghardt DuBois, *The Suppression of the African Slave Trade* (New York: Longmans, Green, 1896), Appendix A, pp. 201–223.
16. *Ibid.*
17. Cited in Phillips (work cited in note 2), p. 100; also in DuBois (work cited in note 15), p. 201.
18. See Gray (work cited in note 1), Vol. I, p. 356.
19. *Ibid.*
20. *Ibid.*, pp. 357–358.
21. *Ibid.*, p. 356.
22. *Ibid.*, p. 358. See also Frederic Bancroft, *Slave Trading in the Old South* (Baltimore: J. H. Furst Co., 1934), pp. 3–4; DuBois (work cited in note 15), Chap. IV.
23. See F. B. Dexter, *Estimates of the Population of the American Colonies* (Worcester, Mass.: Charles Hamilton, 1887): DuBois (work cited in note 15); Stella H. Sutherland, *Population Distribution in Colonial America* (New York: Columbia University Press, 1936); Bancroft (work cited in note 22); Gray (work cited in note 1): see Vol. II, Appendix 39.
24. See DuBois (work cited in note 15), p. 33. He gives as his source George H. Moore, *Notes on the History of Slavery in Massachusetts* (New York; 1866), p. 51. On the prior abolition of slavery in the state, see Phillips (work cited in note 2), p. 119.
25. See, for example, Bancroft (work cited in note 22), p. 5; Sutherland (work cited in note 23), p. 48; DuBois (work cited in note 15), p. 37.
26. Phillips (work cited in note 2), p. 113.
27. Sutherland (work cited in note 23), pp. 47–48. It is to be noted that this author falls into the age-old error of confusing Negroes and slaves, using the two terms interchangeably.
28. Phillips (work cited in note 2), p. 112.

29. *Ibid.,* pp. 118–120.
30. See Phillips (work cited in note 2), pp. 115–118; Matthew T. Mellow, *Early American Views on Negro Slavery* (Boston: Meader Publishing Co., 1934); Arthur Young Lloyd, *The Slavery Controversy, 1831–1860* (Chapel Hill: University of North Carolina Press, 1939), pp. 14–18.
31. Lloyd (work cited in previous note).
32. See C. Vann Woodward, *The Burden of Southern History,* rev. ed. (Baton Rouge, La.: Louisiana State University Press, 1968).
33. Massachusetts Historical Society, *Collections,* Vol. 45, p. 402; cited by Phillips (work cited in note 2), pp. 119–120.
34. See United States Bureau of the Census, *A Century of Population Growth* (Washington: U. S. Government Printing Office, 1909), pp. 142–143.
35. Lloyd (work cited in note 30).
36. *Ibid.,* pp. 13–14. Lloyd cites as one of his sources a Southern anti-abolitionist, Hilary A. Herbert, *The Abolition Movement and Its Consequences* (New York: Charles Scribner's, 1912). The census data are from U. S. Bureau of the Census (source cited in note 33), pp. 47, 222.
37. Cited, with some apology for awkward language in the original from U. S. Census (source indicated in note 33), p. 85.
38. See Lorenzo Dow Turner, *Anti-Slavery Sentiment in American Literature Prior to 1865* (Washington: Association for the Study of Negro Life and History, 1929), Chap. I; Mary Stoughton Locke, *Anti-Slavery in America from the Introduction of the African Slaves to the Prohibition of the Slave Trade (1619–1808),* Radcliff College Memographs No. 11 (Boston: Ginn and Co., 1901), especially Introduction and Chap. I.
39. See DuBois (work cited in note 15), Chap. IV.
40. *Ibid.*
41. The literature is of course voluminous. A good summary is provided by H. A. Wyndham, *The Atlantic and Slavery* (London: Humphrey Milford, Oxford University Press, 1935).
42. Our source is Gray (work cited in note 1), Vol. I, pp. 358–359.
43. *Ibid.*
44. See DuBois (work cited in note 15), Chap. IV.

Chapter II

1. Lewis Cecil Gray, *History of Agriculture in the Southern United States to 1860* (Washington: Carnegie Institution, 1935, 2 vols.), Vol. 5, p. 364.

2. *Ibid.*, Vol. I, pp. 350–351. The factors listed in the text are based on Gray and on Eugene Irving McCormac, "White Servitude in Maryland," *Johns Hopkins University Studies in Historical and Political Science*, Series *XXII*, Nos. 3–4, March, April 1904.

3. James Truslow Adams, *The Epic of America* (Boston: Little, Brown and Co., 1931), p. 156.

4. *Ibid.*

5. *Ibid.*, p. 175.

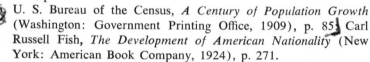

6. U. S. Bureau of the Census, *A Century of Population Growth* (Washington: Government Printing Office, 1909), p. 85; Carl Russell Fish, *The Development of American Nationality* (New York: American Book Company, 1924), p. 271.

7. See William J. Bromwell, *History of Immigration to the United States* (New York: Redfield, 1856), p. 16.

8. See J. D. B. DeBow, *Statistical View of the United States . . . : Compendium of the Seventh Census* (Washington: Beverly Tucker, Senate Printer, 1854), Table XII, p. 121.

9. See Fish (work cited in note 6), p. 271; Bromwell (work cited in note 7), p. 175.

10. Adams (work cited in note 3), p. 157.

11. Cited in Charles A. Beard and Mary R. Beard, *The Rise of American Civilization,* one-vol. ed. (New York: The MacMillan Co., 1930), p. 643 (Vol. I).

12. Arthur Meier Schlesinger, *Political and Social History of the United States,* 1829–1925 (New York: The Macmillan Co., 1926), p. 7.

13. Avery Craven, *The Repressible Conflict* (University, La.: Louisiana State University Press, 1939), p. 45.

14. *Ibid.*, pp. 47–48.

15. Wilbert E. Moore, *Order and Change: Essays in Comparative Sociology* (New York: John Wiley & Sons, 1967), p. 46; see also pp. 19, 65–66.

16. Craven (work cited in note 13), p. 18.

17. Adams (work cited in note 3), p. 182.

18. Schlesinger (work cited in note 12), p. 8.

19. Orestes Brownson in *Boston Quarterly Review*, 3:473, 1840: cited in Helen Sullivan Mims, "Early American Democratic Theory and Orestes Brownson," *Science and Society*, 3: 108–198, Spring, 1939. See also Carter Goodrich and Sol Davidson, "The Wage-earner in the Westward Movement," Political Science Quarterly, 50: 161–185, 1936; 51: 61–116, 1956.
20. Adams (work cited in note 3), p. 179.
21. See Schlesinger (work cited in note 12), pp. 8–10; Beard and Beard (work cited in note 11), Vol. I, pp. 643–647.
22. See Schlesinger (work cited in note 12), pp. 10–15; Beard and Beard (work cited in note 11), Vol. I, pp. 512–545.
23. Adams (work cited in note 3), p. 186.

Chapter III

1. See Lewis Cecil Gray, *History of Agriculture in the Southern United States in 1860* (Washington: Carnegie Institution, 1933), Vol. II, pp. 603–606.
2. *Ibid.,* Vol. II, pp. 602–608. See also M. B. Hammond, "The Cotton Industry: An Essay in American Economic History," *Publications of the American Economic Association,* New Series, No. 1, 1897, pp. 38–40.
3. Gray (work cited in note 1), Vol. II, p. 614.
4. *Ibid.,* Vol. II, p. 616.
5. *Ibid.,* Vol. II, pp. 616–617; Hammond (work cited in note 2), pp. 40–41; U. B. Phillips, *American Negro Slavery* (New York: D. Appleton and Co., 1918), pp. 123–128.
6. Phillips (work cited in preceding note), p. 124.
7. Hammond (work cited in note 2), p. 42; Ulrich B. Phillips, "The Economic Cost of Slaveholding in the Cotton Belt," *Political Science Quarterly,* 20: 257–275 (reprint, Boston: Ginn and Co., 1905).
8. United States Bureau of the Census, *A Century of Population Growth* (Washington: Government Printing Office, 1909), p. 132.
9. See Gray (work cited in note 1), Vol. II, p. 679, Table 22.
10. *Ibid.,* Vol. I, p. 302. See further in Gray, Chaps. XXIII and XXIV, for the best available discussion of plantation organization and management. On this subject the "standard" source on American Negro slavery, Ulrich B. Phillips, is inexcusably prejudiced, anecdotal, and utterly trivial. See his work previously cited (note 5)

and his *Plantation and Frontier* (Cleveland: Arthur W. Clark Co., 1910).

11. I offer here a small set of scholarly citations: ("Agricola"), "Management of Negroes," *De Bow's Review,* 18: 358–363, September 1855; Anon., "Agricultural Department. 1.—Management of Negroes," *ibid.,* 10: 326–328, March 1851; John A. Calhoun, "Management of Slaves," *ibid.,* 18: 713–719, June 1856; St. George Cocke, "Plantation Management.—Police," *ibid.,* 17: 421–426, October 1854; ("A Mississippi Planter"), "Management of Negroes upon Southern Estates," *ibid.,* 10: 621–627, June 1851; (A Small Farmer"), "Management of Negroes," *ibid.,* 11: 369–372, October 1851.

12. Again, in *De Bow's Review,* a shy author: ("A Citizen of Mississippi"), "The Negro," 3: 419, May 1847. For descriptions of family life and conditions among plantation slaves see H. Franklin Frazier, *The Negro Family in the United States* (Chicago, University of Chicago Press, 1939), pp. 23–85.

13. U. B. Phillips (work cited in note 5), pp. 266–267.

14. One small planter reported proudly that he spent $10 annually per hand for such luxuries. See ("A Small Farmer"), "Management of Negroes," *De Bow's Review,* 11: 368–372, October 1851.

15. Gray (work cited in note 1), Vol. I, p. 544.

16. ("A Planter"), "Cotton and Its Cost of Production," *De Bow's Review,* 10: 568–571, May 1851; R. C. Morris, "Slave Labor upon Public Works at the South," *ibid.,* 17: 26–82, July 1854.

17. Gray (work cited in note 1), Vol. I, p. 416.

18. *Ibid.,* pp. 712–714. See also Hammond (work cited in note 2), pp. 107–112.

19. Gray (work cited in note 1).

20. Hammond (work cited in note 2), pp. 43–47.

21. Phillips (work cited in note 5), p. 343; see also p. 339.

22. Phillips, "The Economic Cost of Slaveholding in the Cotton Belt," *Political Science Quarterly,* 20: 257–275 (reprint, Boston: Ginn and Co., 1905).

23. Phillips, "The Origin and Growth of the Southern Black Belts, "*American Historical Review,* 11: 798–816, July, 1906, excerpt from p. 805.

24. Phillips (work cited in note 5), pp. 402–406.

25. See Gray (work cited in note 1), Vol. II, pp. 616, 909, 941.

26. Phillips (work cited in note 22), p. 259.

27. Phillips (work cited in note 23), p. 803.

28. Gray (work cited in note 1), Vol. II, p. 934; see also Vol. I, pp. 470, 566–567.
29. Phillips (work cited in note 5), p. 359.
30. Gray (work cited in note 1), Vol. I, pp. 473–474.
31. *Ibid.,* Vol. I, pp. 471–473.
32. *Ibid.,* Vol. I, pp. 470–471.
33. Phillips (work cited in notes 5, 22, and 23).
34. Hammond (work cited in note 2), Appendix I.
35. Phillips (work cited in note 5), pp. 368–379; also Phillips (work cited in note 22).
36. Phillips (work cited in note 22), p. 270.
37. See Gray (work cited in note 1), Vol. II, p. 650, Table 20. Gray drew in part on W. E. Burghardt DuBois, *The Suppression of the African Slave Trade* (New York: Longman's Green and Co., 1896), pp. 123, 128, 178–182.
38. Gray (work cited in note 1), Vol. II, p. 447.
39. *Ibid.,* p. 448.
40. *Ibid.,* Vol. I, pp. 477–478.
41. *Ibid.,* pp. 447–448.
42. See U. S. Bureau of the Census, *A Century of Population Growth* (Washington: Government Printing Office, 1909), p. 134, Table 62.
43. Phillips (work cited in note 5), figure following p. 370.
44. Phillips (work cited in note 23).
45. See U. B. Phillips, "Plantations with Slave Labor and Free," *American Historical Review,* 30: 798–818, July 1925.
46. Phillips (work cited in note 23), pp. 811–812.
47. Gray (work cited in note 1), Vol. I, p. 482, Table 7, assembled these calculations from U. S. Census sources. Comments are mine, of course.
48. U. B. Phillips, "The Decadence of the Plantation System," Publications of the *American Academy of Political and Social Science,* No. 589 (reprinted from *The Annals* of that Academy, January, 1910, pp. 37–41), excerpt from p. 39.

Chapter IV

1. See Lewis Cecil Gray, *History of Agriculture in the Southern United States to 1860* (Washington: Carnegie Institution, 1933, 2 vols.) Vol. I, pp. 359–360.

2. See John Codman Hurd, *The Law of Freedom and Bondage in the United States* (Boston: Little, Brown and Co.; New York: D. Van Nostrand, 1858, 2 vols.), Vol. I, pp. 159–161.

3. See H. A. Wyndham, *The Atlantic and Slavery* (London: Humphrey Milford, Oxford University Press, 1935), Part III, Chap. I.

4. See Gray (work cited in note 1); Vol. I, p. 360. For a later case involving the slave or free status of a maternal ancestor of the plaintiff, and which was decided on the presumption of slavery as the *status quo ante* of the ancestor in question, see Jacob D. Wheeler, *A Practical Treatise on the Law of Slavery,* New York, Allan Pollock, Jr.; New Orleans, Benjamin Levy, 1837, pp. 11–12. (Negro Mary v. The Vestry of William and Mary's Parish; Oct. T. 1796; 3 Har. and M'Henry's Md. Rep. 501.)

5. See Hurd (work cited in note 2), Vol. I, pp. 161–165.

6. *Ibid.,* Vol. I, pp. 165–170, 210–212, 225–226; also H. W. Jernegan, "Slavery and Conversion in the American Colonies," *American Historical Review,* 21:504–527, April 1916.

7. Cited in Jernegan (work cited in note 6), p. 504.

8. Cited in Hurd (work cited in note 2), Vol. I, p. 232.

9. See H. T. Catterall, *Judicial Cases Concerning American Slavery and the Negro* (Washington: Carnegie Institution of Washington, 1926–1936, 5 vols.), Vol. I (1926), pp. 55–60. This work is the most complete compilation of English and American judicial cases concerning slavery, but its utility for reference is decreased by its arrangement, since cases are arranged by states in the first instance, and in chronological order for each state, rather than by legal questions or principles involved in the slavery system.

10. In addition to the Maryland and Virginia colonial acts, references to which are given in sources cited in notes 7 and 8, the various legislative acts are summarized by state, date, and source. The secondary sources are Jernegan (work cited in note 6) and Hurd work cited in note 2). I regret the length of this note, but it seemed proper to have it on the record.
Virginia
1670: Jernegan, pp. 506–507; Hurd, Vol. I, p. 233.
1682: Jernegan, p. 507; Hurd, Vol. I, pp. 234–235.
1705: Jernegan, p. 507; Hurd, Vol. I, pp. 240–241.
1748: Hurd, Vol. I, p. 243.
Maryland
1671: Jernegan, p. 506.
1692: Hurd, Vol. I, p. 250.

1715: Jernegan, p. 506.
New York
1706: Jernegan, p. 507; Hurd, Vol. I, p. 281.
North Carolina*
1669–1670: Jernegan, p. 507; Hurd, Vol. I, p. 294.
1698: *Ibid.*
South Carolina
1690: Jernegan, p. 507; Hurd, Vol. I, p. 297.
1721: Jernegan, p. 507; Hurd, Vol. I, pp. 300–301.

11. This time, a shorter set of references to colonial legislation, the secondary source being uniformly Hurd (work cited in note 2):
Virginia
1630: Hurd, Vol. I, p. 229.
1670: *Ibid.,* p. 233.
Maryland
1681: *Ibid.,* p. 250.
Massachusetts
1705: *Ibid.,* p. 263.
New Jersey
1713: *Ibid.,* p. 284.

12. *Ibid.,* Vol. I, pp. 159–165.
13. See Wyndham (work cited in note 3).
14. This summary is compiled from citations of colonial legislation in Hurd (work cited in note 2), Vol. I, pp. 228–311. Numbers inserted in the text are page numbers in this secondary source.
15. The source and procedures are the same as those outlined in the preceding note.
16. Explanatory preamble to South Carolina Act of 1712, establishing police regulations governing slaves, cited in Hurd (work cited in note 2), Vol. I, p. 299.
17. Quoted by Wyndham (work cited in note 3), p. 296.
18. Quoted in *ibid.,* pp. 297–298.
19. Quoted, with bracketed insertions, in Hurd (work cited in note 2), p. 207.
20. "Davis (a man of color) v. Curry. Fall T. 1810. 2 Bibb's Rep. 238," (Kentucky), cited in Jacob D. Wheeler, *A Practical Treatise on the Law of Slavery* (New York: Allan Pollock, Jr.; New Orleans, Benjamin Levy, 1837). Cases cited in this chapter are given

---

* This North Carolina Provision is Article 107 of John Locke's *Constitution for the Carolinas.*

as they appear in the collections from which they are cited. The variation in form and punctuation, even in various cases included in the same collection, is therefore not changed.

21. For cases asserting this justification see: "Maria et al. v. Surbaugh. Feb. T. 1825. 2 Rand. Rep. 228," (Virginia), cited in Wheeler (work cited in note 20), p. 5; "Seville v. Chretien. Sept. T. 1817. 5 Martin's Louisiana Rep. 275," in *ibid.*, pp. 8–9; "Hudgins v. Wright. Nov. T. 1806. I. Hen. & Munf. 139." (Virginia) in *ibid.*, p. 12.

22. Cited in Hurd (work cited in note 2), Vol. I, pp. 231–232.

23. *Ibid.*, Vol. I, p. 211.

24. *Ibid.*, Vol. I, pp. 210–211. See also T. R. R. Cobb, *An Inquiry into the Law of Negro Slavery* (Philadelphia: T. and J. W. Johnson and Co.; Savannah: W. Thorne Williams, 1858), Vol. I, pp. 67–70.

25. Maryland from 1664 to 1681 may have been an exception, and, probably, Louisiana during Spanish rule. For the latter exception, see "Re Marie Louise, 14 La. Hist. Q. 598, November 1745," cited in Catterall (work cited in note 9), Vol. III, p. 420.

26. See Hurd (work cited in note 2), Vol. I, p. 165. Mostly from Hurd, I list here the principal laws and cases affirming the hereditary status of slavery. Reference is to a legislative act unless the title of a case is given. Numbers in parentheses are to volumes and pages in Hurd, for laws.

1662. Virginia. (I, 231–232)
1705. Virginia. (I, 240–241)
1706. New York. (I, 281)
1712. South Carolina. (I, 299)
1715. Maryland. (I, 252)
1740. South Carolina. (I, 303)
1760. Delaware. (I, 292)
1785. Virginia. (II, 4)
1806. Virginia. "Hudgins v. Wright, 1 Hen. & Munf. 134," Wheeler (work cited in note 20), p. 3.
1810. Delaware. (II, 78)
1811. Kentucky. "Timm's v. Potter, 1 Haywards' Rep. 234," Wheeler, p. 24.
1825. Louisiana (II, 160–161)

Summaries of cases involving the principle of *partus sequitur ventrem* are also given by Cobb (work cited in note 24), Vol. I, pp. 70–73.

27. The literature on this touchy subject is vast. The standard "modern classic" source is John Dollard, *Caste and Class in a Southern Town* (New Haven: Yale University Press, 1937).

28. Cited in Hurd (work cited in note 2), Vol. I, p. 304.

29. To avoid a page solid with citational notes to cases (so dear to the hearts of lawyers) I note here that they are listed in my article "Slave Law and the Social Structure," *Journal of Negro History*, 24: 171–202, April 1941. My principal secondary sources have been Catterall (work cited in note 9) and Wheeler (work cited in note 20). Short lists of cases involving the presumption of slavery for Negroes are presented in Cobb (work cited in note 24), p. 67, and in C. M. Stroud, *A Sketch of the Laws Relating to Slavery* (Philadelphia: Kimber and Sharpless, 1827).

30. Again, for citation of cases and the variability in the definition of Negroes, see Moore (article cited in preceding note). My principal source, once more, has been Catterall (work cited in note 9).

31. This judgment, quoted at some length, was in the case of "Hudgins v. Wright. Nov. T. 1806. 1 Hen. and Munf. 134," cited in Wheeler (work cited in note 20), pp. 392–394, and in Catterall (work cited in note 9), Vol. I, pp. 112–113. For a listing of further cases, see Moore (article cited in note 29), relying on Catterall.

32. For relevant cases, see sources cited in preceding note.

33. Louisiana Civil Code of 1825, cited in Hurd (work cited in note 2), Vol. II, p. 180.

34. Relevant cases are noted in Wheeler (work cited in note 20), pp. 2 and 37; Catterall (work cited in note 9), Vol. I, p. 103; Hurd (work cited in note 2), Vol. II, p. 195. Full legal citations in Moore (work cited in note 29).

35. See statutes and decisions noted in Hurd (work cited in note 2), Vol. II, p. 5; Catterall (work cited in note 9), Vol. I, pp. 83–84, 86–87; Wheeler (work cited in note 20), pp. 2, 39, 40. Full citations, again, in Moore (work cited in note 29). More extensive citations may also be found by consulting the index of each of the first four volumes of Catterall (work cited in note 9) under "Personal property."

36. For cases see Catterall (work cited in note 9), indexes to the several volumes under "Real estate."

37. For cases see Wheeler (work cited in note 20), pp. 6–7, 191–192.

38. See Cobb (work cited in note 24), Vol. I, pp. lxxii, lxxxviii; also, William Linn Westermann, "Slavery, Ancient," *Encyclopedia of*

the Social Sciences (New York: The Macmillan Co., 1934), Vol. 14, pp. 74–77.

39. For cases, see Catterall (work cited in note 9), indexes to the several volumes under "Manumission, by purchase."

40. For cases, see Catterall (work cited in note 9), Vol. I, p. 307; Vol. II, pp. 146, 217, 232–233, 240, 275–276, 353, 528; Vol. III, pp. 19, 683.

41. See Wheeler (work cited in note 20), p. 190; for cases, see Catterall (work cited in note 9), Vol. II, pp. 203, 308, 468; also Wheeler, pp. 10–11, 190, 237–238.

42. Emile Durkheim, *De la Division du Travail Social* (Paris: Librairie Felix Alcan, 1893), pp. 177–197.

43. See Talcott Parsons, *The Structure of Social Action* (New York: McGraw-Hill Book Co., 1937), p. 312.

44. In chronological order, and with page references to Hurd (work cited in note 2), Vol. II, the state enactments authorizing voluntary enslavement were: Virginia, 1856 (12); Tennessee, 1857 (94); Texas, 1857–1858 (199); Arkansas, 1858–1859 (174); Florida, 1858–1859 (195); Louisiana, 1859 (166); Maryland, 1860 (24).

45. Wheeler (work cited in note 20), p. 197. See in Wheeler also references to state legislation. For citations of relevant judicial decisions, see Catterall (work cited in note 9), Vol. I, pp. 418–419.

46. The relevant cases are cited in Catterall (work cited in note 9), Vol. I, pp. 215–216, 287; Vol. II, pp. 76–77, 221; Vol. III, p. 160. See also Wheeler (work cited in note 20), p. 199.

47. See Cobb (work cited in note 24), p. lxxviii.

48. Kennedy v. Williams, 7 Humphrey's 50, September 1846 [a Tennessee case], in Catterall (work cited in note 9), Vol. II, p. 530.

49. State v. Reed. June T. 1823. 2 Hawk's North Carolina Rep. 454, in Wheeler (work cited in note 20), pp. 210–211.

50. Negro Ann Hammand v. State, 14 Maryland 135, July 1859, in Catterall (work cited in note 9), Vol. IV, p. 139.

51. Jarman v. Patterson, 7 T. B. Mon 644, December 1828 [a Kentucky case], in *ibid.,* Vol. I, p. 311.

52. Catherine Bodine's Will, 4 Dana 476, October 1836 [a Kentucky case], in *ibid.,* Vol. I, pp. 334–335.

53. State v. Jim (a slave), 3 Jones N. C. 348, June 1858 [a North Carolina case], in *ibid.,* Vol. II, p. 198. For other court judg-

ments directly affirming that a slave is a person, see cases in *ibid.*, Vol. I, pp. 122, 149; Vol. III, pp. 167–168, 428, 597, 676; Vol. IV, pp. 224–225.

54. As in notes 10 and 11, I set down here some of the colonial or state legislation, by state and date, the source being uniformly Hurd (work cited in note 2):
    Virginia
    1692: Hurd, Vol. I, pp. 237–238
    1765: *Ibid.*, p. 245
    North Carolina
    1791: *Ibid.*, Vol. II, p. 83
    Delaware
    1827: *Ibid.*, p. 79

55. Baker v. State, 15 Ga. 498, July 1854 [a Georgia case], in Catterall (work cited in note 9), Vol. III, p. 35. For other cases see *ibid.*, Vol. II, pp. 241, 277, 313–314.

56. Cresswell's Executor v. Walker, 37 Ala. 229, January 1861, in *ibid.*, Vol. III, pp. 247–248.

57. The State v. Jim, a negro slave. Dec. T. 1826. 1 Devereaux's North Carolina Rep. 142, in Wheeler (work cited in note 20), pp. 212–213. Again, a brief summary of legislative acts, by state and date, the source being Hurd (work cited in note 2):
    Virginia
    1705: Hurd, Vol. I, pp. 238–239, 241
    1748: *Ibid.*, p. 244
    Texas
    1852: *Ibid.*, Vol. II, p. 199

58. State v. Davis, 14 La. An 678, July 1859 [a Louisiana case], in Catterall (work cited in note 9), Vol. III, p. 674.

59. State v. Hale. Dec. T. 1823. 2 Hawk's North Carolina Rep. 582, in Wheeler (work cited in note 20), pp. 240–242.

60. Again, a summary of legislative acts, by state and date, the source being Hurd (work cited in note 2):
    South Carolina
    1690: Hurd, Vol. I, p. 297
    1740: *Ibid.*, p. 306
    North Carolina
    1817: *Ibid.*, Vol. II, p. 85
    For judicial decisions, see Catterall (work cited in note 9), Vol. II, pp. 356, 494; Vol. III, p. 233. See also Wheeler (work cited

in note 20), pp. 252–254. For a general discussion of this point of law, from the point of view of an abolitionist, see Stroud (work cited in note 29), pp. 35–44.

61. The State v. Mann. Dec. T. 1829. 2 Devereaux's North Carolina Rep. 263, in Wheeler (work cited in note 20), pp. 245–248.

62. Virginia Act of 1689, in Hurd (work cited in note 2), Vol. I, p. 232. Other colonial or state acts, by state and date, the source being Hurd unless otherwise noted:

Virginia
1723: Hurd, Vol. I, p. 242
South Carolina
1690: *Ibid.,* p. 297
North Carolina
1798: Stroud (work cited in note 29), p. 37
Tennessee
1799: Hurd, Vol. II, p. 90

63. Stroud (work cited in note 29), p. 38.

64. See Virginia Act of 1723 in Hurd (work cited in note 2), Vol. I, p. 242. Also State v. Tackett, 1 Hawks 210, December 1820 [a North Carolina case], in Catterall (work cited in note 9), Vol. II, pp. 39–40.

65. Another brief summary of legislative acts, by colony or state and date, the source being once more Hurd (work cited in note 2):

Virginia
1680: Hurd, Vol. I, p. 234
1705: *Ibid.,* p. 241
1748: *Ibid.,* p. 244
Tennessee
1799: *Ibid.,* Vol. II, p. 90
Georgia
1816: *Ibid.,* p. 103
Alabama
1819: *Ibid.,* p. 150
Florida
1828: *Ibid.,* p. 192

66. The State v. Manar. Spring T. 1834. 2 Hill's Rep. 453 [a South Carolina case], in Wheeler (work cited in note 20), p. 243. Other relevant cases are cited by Wheeler at pp. 239, 243, 249.

67. Legislative provisions are summarized by Wheeler (work cited in note 20), p. 194, and a relevant South Carolina case at pp. 193–194.

Chapter V

1. Cited in U. B. Phillips, *American Negro Slavery* (New York: D. Appleton and Co., 1918), p. 150; see also pp. 283–286.
2. D. R. Hundley, *Social Relations in Our Southern States* (New York: Henry B. Price, 1860), Chap. III.
3. *Ibid.,* p. 132.
4. See Vernon Louis Parrington, *Main Currents in American Thought* (New York: Harcourt, Brace and Co., 1927, 2 vols.), Vol. II, *The Romantic Revolution in America,* pp. 99–108.
5. Phillips (work cited in note 1), Chaps XIV and XV.
6. Theodore Weld, *American Slavery as It Is: Testimony of a Thousand Witnesses* (New York: American Anti-Slavery Society, 1839).
7. *Ibid.,* pp. 62–84. The punctuation and italics are all as they occur in Weld's lists. It may safely be assumed that he has added the emphasis to the original advertisements to fit his propaganda purposes. The lists given in the pages cited include 196 such items.
8. See B. W. Doyle, *The Etiquette of Race Relations in the South* (Chicago: University of Chicago Press, 1937).
9. Hundley (work cited in note 2), p. 170.
10. Lewis Cecil Gray, *History of Agriculture in the Southern United States to 1860* (Washington: Carnegie Institution, 1933, 2 vols.), Vol. I, pp. 518–519.
11. See W. D. Weatherford, *The Negro from Africa to America* (New York: George H. Doran Co., 1924), pp. 145–146.
12. I borrow these conceptual distinctions from Talcott Parsons, *The Social System* (Glencoe, Ill.: Free Press, 1951), especially pp. 45–112.
13. Pitirim A. Sorokin, *Social and Cultural Dynamics* (New York: American Book Co., 1937–1940, 4 vols.), Vol. III, p. 37.
14. *Ibid.,* pp. 24–30.
15. Phillips (who was almost exclusively concerned with the familistic type of relationship) may be consulted for a general description of plantation life associated with this general type. See his *American Negro Slavery* (cited in note 1), Chaps. XV and XVI, and *Life and Labor in the Old South* (Boston: Little, Brown and Co., 1929), Chaps. XI–XIII.
16. Hundley (work cited in note 2), pp. 352–353.

17. See Phillips, *Life and Labor in the Old South* (cited in note 15).
18. See Phillips (work cited in notes 1 and 15).
19. Unpublished lecture cited by Doyle (work cited in note 8), pp. 198–199.
20. From Gray (work cited in note 10), Vol. I, p. 482, Table 7; original data from U. S. census sources.
21. *Ibid.*
22. Hundley (work cited in note 2), Chaps. I and IV.
23. Gray (work cited in note 10), Vol. I, pp. 492–497.
24. Roger W. Shugg, *Origins of Class Struggle in Louisiana* (University, La.: Louisiana State University Press, 1939), p. 32.
25. Concerning the yeomen, see Hundley (work cited in note 2), Chap. V, and Phillips, *Life and Labor in the Old South* (cited in note 15), Chap. XVII. Concerning White artisans, see Gray (work cited in note 10), Vol. I, pp. 500–501. "Highlanders" are briefly described in Gray, Vol. I, pp. 487–488.
26. See Frederic Bancroft, *Slave-Trading in the Old South* (Baltimore: J. H. Furst Co., 1934), pp. 365–381.
27. *Ibid.*
28. Gray (work cited in note 10), Vol. I, p. 521.
29. See especially Paul H. Buck, "The Poor Whites of the Ante-Bellum South," *American Historical Review,* 31: 41–54, October 1925.
30. Dollard is thus quite clearly mistaken when he views the Negro-White caste system as a post-war development, and as a substitute for the slavery system. See John Dollard, *Caste and Class in a Southern Town* (New Haven: Yale University Press, 1937), pp. 62–63.
31. See E. B. Reuter, *The Mulatto in the United States* (Boston: Richard G. Badger, 1918), pp. 105–126.
32. See E. Senart, *Caste in India* (London: Methuen and Co., 1930).
33. *Ibid.,* pp. 169–174.
34. Avery Craven, *The Repressible Conflict,* 1830–1861 (University, La.: Louisiana State University Press, 1939), p. 59.
35. Adapted from a similar diagram originally prepared by Robin M. Williams, Jr., in an unpublished paper, and subsequently published in our joint paper: Wilbert E. Moore and Robin M. Williams, Jr., "Stratification in the Ante-Bellum South," *American Sociological Review,* 7:343–351, June 1942.
36. D. L. Dumond, *Antislavery Origins of the Civil War in the*

United States (Ann Arbor: University of Michigan Press, 1939), p. 13.

37. Gray (work cited in note 10), Vol. I, pp. 520–521.

38. Phillips, *American Negro Slavery* (cited in note 1), pp. 291, 339, and elsewhere.

39. Hundley (work cited in note 2), pp. 342–347.

40. Doyle (work cited in note 8), pp. 68–80.

41. See Phillips, *American Negro Slavery* (cited in note 1), pp. 24–25, 41–44, 301–305.

42. Weld (work cited in note 6) gives long lists of advertisements, selected, like the samples quoted earlier in the chapter, to illustrate various anti-slavery arguments.

43. Herbert Aptheker, *Negro Slave Revolts in the United States, 1526–1860* (New York: International Publishers, 1939).

44. For sake of brevity, specific citations will not be given to the various laws. All are cited in John Codman Hurd, *The Law of Freedom and Bondage in the United States* (Boston: Little, Brown and Co.; New York: D. Van Nostrand, 1858), 2 vols.

45. Dumond (work cited in note 36), p. 13.

46. See Herbert Aptheker, *The Negro in the Civil War* (New York: International Publishers, 1938).

47. Phillips, *American Negro Slavery* (cited in note 1), p. 396.

48. For examples, see William Sumner Jenkins, *Pro-Slavery Thought in the Old South* (Chapel Hill: University of North Carolina Press, 1935).

49. Cited in Jenkins (reference in preceding note), Chap. VI. Dr. Mott's work was self-styled as "niggerology."

50. *Ibid.,* pp. 247–248.

51. Cited in *ibid.,* pp. 122–130.

Chapter VI

1. See Lorenzo Dow Turner, *Anti-Slavery Sentiment in American Literature Prior to 1865* (Washington: Association for the Study of Negro Life and History, 1929); Mary Stoughton Locke, *Anti-Slavery in America from the Introduction of the African Slaves to the Prohibition of the Slave Trade (1619–1808)*, Radcliffe College Monographs No. 11 (Boston: Ginn and Co., 1901).

2. See Locke, *Anti-Slavery in America from the Introduction of the*

African Slaves to the Prohibition of the Slave Trade (1619–1808), p. 21.

3. *Ibid.,* p. 1.
4. *Ibid.,* pp. 109–169.
5. See Alice Dana Adams, *The Neglected Period of Anti-Slavery in America,* Radcliffe College Monographs No. 14 (Boston and London: Ginn and Co., 1908), p. 106.
6. See Thomas Earl, ed., *The Life, Travels, and Opinions of Benjamin Lundy* (Philadelphia: William D. Parrish, 1847).
7. Adams, *The Neglected Period of Anti-Slavery in America,* p. 137.
8. Quoted in Vernon Louis Parrington, *Main Currents in American Thought; Vol. II, The Romantic Revolution in America* (New York: Harcourt, Brace and Co., 1927), p. 354.
9. As reported in the *Third Annual Report,* 1836, of the American Anti-Slavery Society, and cited by W. Sherman Savage, *The Controversy over the Distribution of Abolition Literature, 1830–1860* (Washington: The Association for the Study of Negro Life and History, 1938), p. 13.
10. See Parrington, *Main Currents in American Thought; Vol. II, The Romantic Revolution in America,* pp. 359–360.
11. See Albert Bushnell Hart, *Slavery and Abolition* (New York: Harper and Bros., 1906), pp. 170–201.
12. See Turner, *Anti-Slavery Sentiment in American Literature prior to 1865,* Chap. I; also Locke, *Anti-Slavery in America from the Introduction of the African Slaves to the Prohibition of the Slave Trade (1619–1808).*
13. Published in *Massachusetts Historical Society Collections,* 5th Series, Vol. VI.
14. Horace Mann, *Speech on the Right of Congress to Legislate for the Territories of the United States, and Its Duty to Exclude Slavery Therefrom* (Washington: J. and G. S. Gideon, 1848). Delivered, U. S. House of Representatives, June 30, 1848.
15. See William I. Bowditch, *Slavery and the Constitution* (Boston: Robert F. Wallcut, 1849); also Mann, *Speech on the Right of Congress to Legislate for the Territories of the United States, and Its Duty to Exclude Slavery Therefrom;* also Andrew P. Peabody, *Position and Duties of the North with Regard to Slavery* (Newburyport: Charles Whipple, 1847).
16. See Peabody, *Position and Duties of the North with Regard to Slavery.*

17. Theodore Weld's *American Slavery as It Is: Testimony of a Thousand Witnesses* (New York: American Anti-Slavery Society, 1839) is replete with descriptions and charges of immorality resulting from the debasing effects of slavery.

18. See William I. Bowditch, *The Anti-Slavery Reform, Its Principle and Method* (Boston: Robert F. Wallcut, 1850).

19. See Arthur Young Lloyd, *The Slavery Controversy, 1831–1860* (Chapel Hill: University of North Carolina Press, 1939), pp. 162–193.

20. Mann, *Speech on the Right of Congress to Legislate for the Territories of the United States, and Its Duty to Exclude Slavery Therefrom.*

21. See Bowditch, *Slavery and the Constitution.*

22. See Mann, *Speech on the Right of Congress to Legislate for the Territories of the United States, and Its Duty to Exclude Slavery Therefrom.*

23. See Turner, *Anti-Slavery Sentiment in American Literature prior to 1865.*

24. See Albert K. Weinberg, *Manifest Destiny, a Study of Nationalist Expansion in American History* (Baltimore: The Johns Hopkins Press, 1935).

25. Cited in *Report of the Arguments of Counsel, and the Opinion of the Court, in the Case of Commonwealth vs. Aves. . . .* (Boston: Isaac Knapp, 1836).

26. See American Anti-Slavery Society, "Disunion, an Address . . . on the Pro-Slavery Character of the Constitution," *Anti-Slavery Examiner* [Vol. I], No. 12, New York, 1845.

27. See R[alph] W[aldo] Emerson, *An Address Delivered in the Court-House in Concord, Massachusetts on 1st August, 1814, on the Anniversary of the Emancipation of the Negroes in the British West Indies* (Boston: James Munroe and Co., 1844); also [John G.] Palfrey, *Speech on the Political Aspect of the Slave Question* (Washington: J. and G. S. Gideon, 1848). (Delivered, U. S. House of Representatives, January 26, 1848).

28. Mann, Horace, *Speech . . . on the Subject of Slavery in the Territories and the Consequences of a Dissolution of the Union* (Boston: Redding and Co., 1850). (Delivered, U. S. House of Representatives, 1850.)

29. See Turner, *Anti-Slavery Sentiment in American Literature prior to 1865,* Chap. I.

30. See Mann, *Speech on the Right of Congress to Legislate for the Territories of the United States, and Its Duty to Exclude Slavery Therefrom.*

31. See [John G.] Palfrey, *Speech on the Bill Creating a Territorial Government for Upper California* (Washington, no. pub., 1849). (Delivered, U. S. House of Representatives, February 26, 1849.)

32. See Mann, *Speech on the Right of Congress to Legislate for the Territories of the United States, and Its Duty to Exclude Slavery Thereform* and *Speech . . . on the Subject of Slavery in the Territories and the Consequences of a Dissolution of the Union.*

33. Turner, *Anti-Slavery Sentiment in American Literature prior to 1865,* p. 18.

34. *Ibid.,* p. 89.

35. Quoted as an extract of a letter from Mr. W. Dustin to Theodore Weld in the latter's *American Slavery as It Is: Testimony of a Thousand Witnesses,* p. 65.

36. Quoted from Mr. Samuel Ball, a teacher in Marietta College, Ohio, in *ibid.,* p. 69.

37. *Ibid.,* pp. 169–170. Italics and capitals have been omitted from Weld's quotation from the prospectus, as undoubtedly added by him and not in the original.

38. See Turner, *Anti-Slavery Sentiment in American Literature prior to 1865.*

39. Massachusetts Anti-Slavery Society, *A Full Statement of the Reasons . . . Why There Should Be No Penal Laws Enacted . . . Respecting Abolitionists and Anti-Slavery Societies* (Boston: Printed by Isaac Knapp for the Society, 1836); excerpt from p. 18.

40. See, for example, Emerson, *An Address Delivered in the Court-House in Concord, Massachusetts on 1st August, 1814, on the Anniversary of the Emancipation of the Negroes in the British West Indies.*

41. Arguments marked with an asterisk (*) definitely assume an ethical valuation of the individual; those marked with the sign (#) may do so, depending on the context. Others have no apparent relation to that central issue.

42. See Hart, *Slavery and Abolition,* pp. 197–201.

43. *Proceedings of the [Second] Anti-Slavery Convention of American Women Held in Philadelphia* (Philadelphia: Printed by Merrihew and Gunn, 1838).

44. See Carl Russell Fish, *The Rise of the Common Man* (New York: The Macmillan Co., 1927).

45. Frank J. Klingberg, *The Anti-Slavery Movement in England* (New Haven: Yale University Press, 1926), p. 25.
46. See D. L. Dumond, *Antislavery Origins of the Civil War in the United States* (Ann Arbor: University of Michigan Press, 1939), pp. 51–61; also Savage, *The Controversy over the Distribution of Abolition Literature, 1830–1860,* pp. 31–33.
47. A. E. Grimke, "Appeal to the Christian Women of the South," *The Anti-Slavery Examiner,* Vol. I, No. 2, September 1836; excerpt from p. 23.
48. *Ibid.,* p. 30.
49. See Lloyd, *The Slavery Controversy, 1831–1860,* pp. 139–150.
50. Quoted from Greeley's *Hints toward Reforms* by Parrington, *Main Currents in American Thought*; Vol. II, *The Romantic Revolution in America,* pp. 256–257.
51. Avery Craven, *The Repressible Conflict, 1830–1861* (University, La.: Louisiana State University Press, 1939), pp. 34–35.
52. *Ibid.,* p. 57.

INDEX